Pheasant
Days

Pheasant Days

CHRIS DORSEY

Foreword by Craig Boddington

VOYAGEUR PRESS

Printed in the United States of America
First hardcover edition
91 92 93 94 95 5 4 3 2 1
First softcover edition
94 95 96 97 98 5 4 3 2 1

Library of Congress Cataloging-in-Publication Data

Dorsey, Chris, 1965–
Pheasant days / Chris Dorsey ; foreword by Craig Boddington
p.   cm.
Includes bibliographical references and index.
ISBN 0-89658-170-5
ISBN 0-89658-259-0 (pbk.)
1. Pheasant shooting. 2. Ring-necked pheasant. I. Title.
SK325.P5D67   1992
799.2'48617—dc20
91-42276
CIP

Published by
VOYAGEUR PRESS, INC.
123 North Second Street, P.O. Box 338
Stillwater, MN 55082 U.S.A.
612-430-2210, toll-free 800-888-9653

Distributed in Canada by
RAINCOAST BOOKS
112 East Third Avenue
Vancouver, B.C. V5T 1C8

Voyageur Press books are also available at discounts for quantities for educational, fundraising,
premium, or sales-promotion use. For details contact the marketing department. Please write or
call for our free catalog of natural history and outdoor publications.

To retired bird dogs—like my sleepy setter,

Thor—whose paws still twitch

when they dream of pheasants

Contents

Acknowledgments

I stand in debt to many people for their assistance in producing this book. The composite personalities of all the pheasant hunters I have ever known stood over my shoulder while I wrote this book, editing and flavoring my thoughts with every keystroke. Some, but not all, of those people include favorite hunting partners the likes of Gary Wilson, Keith Gilbertson, Phil Brodbeck, Steve Ballentine, Chuck Petrie, Mike Pearce, and Pat Babbitt—hunters who all share the same reverence for ringnecks.

Three pheasant experts—Dr. Richard Warner, Steve Grooms, and Jeff Finden—provided insightful analysis about the future of American pheasant hunting. Countless biologists also volunteered essential research data that helped paint the portrait of the ringneck in America—to them I tip my hat in gratitude.

Eleven outstanding photographers contributed their works to this book: Ron Spomer, Herb Lange, Mark Kayser, Bob Queen, Denver Bryan, Don Bates, Peter Squibb, Keith Benoist, Milt Friend, Stan Warren, and the late Dave Hetzler. This project would not have been complete without them. The South Dakota Tourism Office and the Wisconsin and Michigan Departments of Natural Resources were also exceedingly generous with their files of pheasant photography. Moreover, historian Ann Jenks of the South Dakota Historical Society worked expeditiously to provide snapshots from the past. It was also never too late nor too early to call upon the computer troubleshooting of my sister-in-law, Kathy Dorsey. Without her patience, this book would still be stuck somewhere in the recesses of a computer memory bank.

Lastly, authors Lionel Atwill, Robert McCabe, George Burger, Steve Smith, Dave Duffey, Aldo Leopold, Datus Proper, Tom Davis, and Durward Allen all contributed wit and wisdom in the form of selected quotes. Their words help define the pursuit of pheasant hunting, the moments of awesome elation as well as reflective concern for the future of the sport.

Foreword

The cackling, wing-beating, mind-numbing flush of a rooster pheasant—especially an unknown bird you have trod near—is not for the faint of heart. Whether it's experienced for the first time or the thousandth, that explosion—often from cover that seemingly wouldn't conceal a field mouse—simply can't help but start a powerful surge of adrenalin. And even in experienced hunters who should know better, the noise and suddenness of a surprise flush is likely to produce hand-freezing, chest-tightening panic!

I'll never forget the first time it happened to me. It was along a low ridge in western Kansas, where a wheat field met a weedy edge. I'd shot at some birds, flushed by others, that happened to come my way, so I thought I was a pheasant hunter. But I wanted one of those long-tailed iridescent birds all to myself, and I thought I knew exactly how to handle it. I didn't.

I'd taken a step past the hidden bird, then by pure chance had paused to make sure I was still aligned—as my dad had taught me—with the hunters on either side. Then, with my left foot out-stretched to take another step, the rooster came up to my right, cackling as he clawed for altitude. He was indeed all mine; no one else was around, and in the afternoon sun there was no question whether this was a hen or a cock. I remember his white neck ring, eye-level at six feet, and the blur of his wings.

To my credit, I got my left foot back on the ground, and somehow twisted enough of my body around to bring up the Model 12, big and a touch awkward for me in those days. I even got the safety off and fired my three shells in the bird's general direction. And then I watched him fly unscathed toward the far horizon while my heartbeat slowly returned to normal.

The special excitement that only we hunters feel is a large part of why we do what we do, and this our long-tailed bird offers in unusual measure. With experience, we learn to control the panic when a pheasant flushes—but no hunter ever loses the surge of excitement.

It's amazing how this gaudy Chinese import has become such an important part of America's hunting heritage. They came in at a time when still-unsophisticated farming practices were ideal for them to increase their range and multiply, and in the century since their first introduction we've seen their numbers wax and wane as our land uses changed.

My father's father had the passion for the hunt that I inherited, and in his day in the Midwest hunters hunted birds. My father remembers tagging along with his father in the Dust Bowl days of the thirties, when game was scarce in our native Kansas. Then Franklin Roosevelt's Soil Bank, designed to prevent the Dust Bowl's wind erosion, set aside vast acreage that provided needed habitat. Bird populations exploded. My dad often recalls his first trip to South Dakota in 1942, just before he left for the Navy. He tells of a sky black with pheasants at the end of every stubble field, a sight my generation of hunters has never seen.

The long war gave the birds a rest from hunting pressure, and indeed many fields lay fallow with much of the work force in uniform or in factories producing war materiel. Hunters in the late forties and fifties almost certainly experienced the finest upland hunting this continent has ever offered, but by the time my—and

Chris Dorsey's—generation came along in the sixties and seventies things had changed again.

Killer winters, a gradual but consistent increase in hunting pressure, and loss of habitat as land uses changed and farming became more intensive, made my dad's clouds of pheasants a thing of the past. I walked a long way on that sunny Kansas day of thirty years ago before I flushed my first pheasant—and I would walk much farther before I had another bird all to myself!

Of course, game populations are dynamic, responding well to favorable conditions. Thanks not so much to enlightened management but rather to a series of mild winters, in the late sixties and early seventies we enjoyed an unbelievable plenty of the long-tailed bird in those endless Kansas stubble fields. But bad winters came in succession, and farming became even more intensive. Just a decade ago, when I'd go home for a visit, it seemed the walks between flushes were as long as they'd been when I was a boy.

Today things are changing again. There's a greatly increased awareness of the meaning of that all-important word, HABITAT—and with government programs like the Conservation Reserve Program (CRP) in place, and private groups like Pheasants Forever increasing in influence, the future seems brighter than ever. No, I don't think I'll ever see my dad's clouds of pheasants, nor will Chris Dorsey. But we've both endured those long walks between flushes—and in the nineties, as those walks become shorter, we'll appreciate each and every raucous flush.

It's been my pleasure to work with Chris Dorsey for the past several years. He's a good hand with a rifle, and he's a fine target shot at any shotgun game. He's unusually skilled with his camera, and he's also one of the most talented writers I know. But I've come to realize that his true passion is bird hunting—and thanks to his unusual talents, you'll share that passion as you turn these pages.

I think you'll find that this tribute to the long-tailed bird will not only stir memories of flushes past, but prepare you for the moment when that bright-feathered wonder explodes from cover underneath you—and help you to shorten the walks between those brilliant moments. I know you'll enjoy it—almost as much as walking the edge of a stubble field on a frosty pheasant morning.

CRAIG BODDINGTON, EDITOR, PETERSEN'S *HUNTING*

Introduction

"THE CASE FOR A LAND ETHIC WOULD APPEAR HOPELESS BUT FOR THE
MINORITY WHICH IS IN OBVIOUS REVOLT AGAINST THESE
'MODERN' TRENDS."—ALDO LEOPOLD, A SAND COUNTY ALMANAC

Introduction
Are Pheasants Forever?

Pheasant hunting is about passion. It's about living life the way it was meant to be lived—on the land and by the land. At the center of the sport's allure is the bird itself. The ringneck is three pounds of feathered rainbow, dressed in plumage that, at first look, you are sure contains all the colors in the spectrum. For that reason, the pheasant is a paradox: Its appearance suggests that it was made to be noticed, yet it spends much of its life trying to go unnoticed.

Pheasant hunting, like life itself, is often a search for the unknown. What lies ahead? How do you find it? Are you ready? Every hunt brings new questions, making the sport more compelling with every step into pheasant country. We know much about the pheasant, but it's what we don't know that fuels our addiction to its pursuit. In its elemental form, "... hunting is such a universal and impassioned sport," wrote Spanish philosopher Jose Ortega y Gasset, "that it belongs in the repertory of the purest forms of human happiness."

It isn't so much that pheasants are important, it is what they represent that is so valuable. They connect us to our past like some sort of time machine, reviving lost moments spent with special friends and family. I am not a subsistence hunter by definition, yet I know that I obtain great nourishment from the hunt. The exhilaration of watching the pup that I raised and trained scent a pheasant, point it, and ultimately retrieve the bird is perhaps as important to my physical being as any meat derived from the experience. The pheasant occupies a special niche on the land and

Controlled burns impede the growth of woody cover into prime nesting grasslands. Such burns are often conducted in early spring, before pheasant nesting begins. (Photo © by Bob Queen)

The rapid growth of Pheasants Forever has sparked renewed confidence that North American pheasant populations can rebound from the lows of the 1970s. (Photo © by Mark Kayser, South Dakota Tourism)

in my mind—reason enough, I suppose, to dedicate so much of my life to chasing it.

The pheasant, too, is a bird by which we can gauge the health of our rural landscape. It, like the miner's canary, provides a living barometer of environmental conditions. Farmland set-asides spawned from the 1985 and 1990 Farm Bills and their offshoot, the Conservation Reserve Program (CRP), have proven how quickly game populations can rebound if only given a place to live. The CRP was designed to slow the nation's loss of valuable topsoil by allowing cover to grow on the land for several years, and its indirect benefit to wildlife was, and has been, measured by a steady increase in farmland wildlife. Where once the plains were endless seas of corn and wheat, there are now fallow fields offering sorely needed habitat to animals.

It took an enlightened view by conservationists, farmers, and legislators to understand that everyone has a vested interest in a living environment. For the first time, that view was received in Washington, D.C., because years of American overproduction left grain rotting in elevators from Omaha to New Orleans. At last, it was recognized that we no longer needed to assault the landscape in order to extract every possible grain of wheat or kernel of corn.

The CRP rekindled memories of another similar farmland set-aside program—the Soil Bank of the 1950s. It was a time when hunters and their dogs had unlimited places to find pheasants, quail, and rabbits throughout the grass-strewn fields of America's farm belt. The virtue of such places doesn't lie so much in numbers of birds harvested, but in the memories of flushes that revisit us. I can't drive through farm country without thinking of my first pup—part Brittany, part Labrador, but mostly bird crazy. With the sound of a sparrow flying from a bush along a city street, I am instantly transported to a southern Wisconsin marsh where I watched, for the first time, a rooster pheasant thunder into the sky, blowing the calm from the moment as it crudely yodeled its way skyward.

Such wild places change people. Thoreau held the pen while the muses of Walden wrote. For hunters, it isn't the potential targets that wild places harbor that are especially significant, it is the opportunities they offer to teach people that there is more to a swamp than mud and water, that there is value to land even if a shopping mall or high rise can't be built upon it. As noted conservationist Aldo Leopold wrote in his now immortalized *A Sand County Almanac,* "There is much confusion between land and country. Land is the place where corn, gullies, and mortgages grow. Country is the personality of land, the collective harmony of its soil, life, and weather." It is the land's ability to be country, I think, that must endure.

I wonder what kind of person I would have become if I had never been given a bird dog nor handed a shotgun with plenty of country to roam. What if I hadn't the opportunity to wander meadows and marshes with a hell-bent pup and a single-shot 20-gauge? I would never have come to know so many farmers, their concern for their families and the future of their land. Nor would I know the satisfaction of being a part of the wild community, instead of merely an intruder. I wouldn't have learned to hop a creek without getting wet, nor would I know how to find grubs for ice-fishing in the stems of goldenrod. Indeed, I am only now realizing how much I owe to country.

I now know that I would never trade the path that I have chosen. I find comfort in knowing where to find a pheasant track in the snow and how to turn it into a flush, then a meal, and ultimately a memory.

Walking the road less traveled, to paraphrase Frost, is a process of filtering through life's experiences to discover what is truly worthwhile. Learning the personality of country and its parts—winding roads, crowing pheasants, and sweeping pastures—becomes

The future of pheasant hunting. By securing critical nesting cover, Pheasants Forever has been assisting state agencies with vital habitat and research studies. (Photo © by Pete Squibb)

a life-long passion because it is worthwhile. To look at land and only see pheasants per acre is to not see the value of country. You manage people, you don't manage pheasants. You accept them as part of a healthy countryside, and manage those who don't see the virtue in sharing the landscape with them. If we can preserve country in our hearts, and all that goes with it, perhaps we can save it on the land. Perhaps.

An American Immigrant

"THE BEAUTY OF THE LIVING WORLD I WAS TRYING TO SAVE HAS ALWAYS BEEN UPPERMOST IN MY MIND—THAT, AND AN ANGER AT THE SENSELESS, BRUTISH THINGS THAT WERE BEING DONE. . . ."
—RACHEL CARSON, SILENT SPRING

An American Immigrant
Adding to the Melting Pot

A HISTORIC BIRD

Perhaps our fascination with pheasants lies in the similarity we, as Americans, have with them. Though they never walked the halls of Ellis Island, pheasants are imports like the rest of us. While some came on ships from China, others arrived from England, having captured the interest of Americans as early as 1733.

It was in that year that the first recorded attempt to introduce the birds to North America occurred. Then New York governor Colonel John Montgomerie released twelve pairs of black-necked birds onto Nutten Island, New York. The effort failed, and biologists later speculated that the birds were genetically inferior, having lost the needed wildness to survive because they were the progeny of birds that had spent generations of life in British aviaries. The birds, very likely, were little more than very colorful leghorns. It was Benjamin Franklin's son-in-law, Richard Bach, who was the next to try in 1790. Although records don't show how many birds he released in New Jersey, his attempt, too, was a failure. It was said that even George Washington, during his first term as president, ordered several pairs of pheasants sent from England to his famed Mount Vernon estate in Virginia.

It wasn't until 1882, however, when Judge Owen Denny, then consul-general at Shanghai, brought eight pheasants to America. Some birds died en route during the rough voyage to the New World, the rest perished shortly after arriving at port in Seattle, Washington. Undaunted by his initial failure, the judge sent sixty

Through a series of successful stocking programs across much of the northern half of America, pheasants gradually found a niche in the friendly landscape of the New World. (Photo © by Pete Squibb)

more birds stateside. This time, he had them shipped to Portland, Oregon, where the birds were ultimately released at Denny's homestead in the Willamette Valley in Linn County, Oregon. This was one of the earliest introductions of true Chinese ringnecks to America.

Most of the previous stockings were done with birds from Europe, some that had been descendants of birds raised in captivity for some nine hundred years. According to Echard's *History of England,* pheasants were first brought to Britain by the Romans in 1299 A.D. Clearly the birds have long fascinated people from early intrepid explorers to modern day wingshooters.

Later, in 1892, the "Denny" pheasants, as locals had come to call them, were abundant enough in the valley that a seventy-five-day hunting season was established for them. Ironically, pheasants gained their first foothold in America on the west coast, despite all previous efforts to introduce the birds in the East. By 1907, at least isolated populations of pheasants had taken hold in thirty-nine states.

The birds made piecemeal gains across the continent, ever-increasing their presence on the land and in the hearts of the American hunter. By the start of World War II, pheasants occupied most of the range in which they are currently found in North America. The middle of the 1940s saw the heyday for pheasants in America. Biologist Robert Dahlgren in his report, "Distribution and Abundance of the Ring-Necked Pheasant in North America," emphasized this when he wrote, "The continental harvest of pheasants today barely exceeds the kill of pheasants reported from North and South Dakota in 1945." A survey by the Fish and Wildlife Service in 1940 further underscored the rapid growth of interest hunters had in the pheasant. The survey tallied that there were roughly 2,030 licensed game breeders across North America who were raising pheasants.

Pheasants, historically, have never fared well in the South. They seem, instead, to prefer cover above the line of 40 degrees north latitude. Much of our best grain-producing regions lie north of that delineation. Not surprisingly, then, pheasant populations in America have risen and ebbed around farming practices. Pheasants have traditionally thrived in the absence of intensive agriculture, but make no mistake, they do best when there is a harmony among the plow, cropfields, fencelines, and marshes.

THE EARLY STUDIES

The importance of agriculture to pheasants wasn't documented until research money was made available courtesy of a self-imposed tax by hunters that was enacted in 1937. The new surcharge, called the Pittman-Robertson Tax after its congressional sponsors, cre-ated funding that benefited all types of wildlife research and management—albeit much of the early research lacked hard scientific backing. Habitat management, and the nuances of what it meant to pheasants, was in its fledgling stages in the 1930s and 1940s.

The conventional wisdom of the day, however, suggested that refuges were important to sustaining pheasants and other wildlife. The theory implied that these refuges would protect enough seed stock to replenish adjacent areas that could be overharvested during hunting seasons. Later research concluded, however, that this "refuge effect" never actually existed.

During the early 1940s, it was also widely accepted that stocking cock pheasants in the spring was a good way to ensure enough mates for existing hen populations. By the end of the decade, though, researchers had already determined that such efforts were to little effect. One rooster, it was learned, could service several hens, thus there wasn't a need to provide additional cocks in the population.

Not all early beliefs, however, were misguided. Trapping and transplanting wild pheasants to new areas as a way to establish pheasant flocks—a technique still employed by wildlife agencies today—got its start in Ohio in the 1940s. This technique has been used with great success to expand populations of other species as well. The recent resurgence of the wild turkey across the continent, for example, has been achieved largely through capture and relocation operations.

Several states have entered into swap arrangements—trading one species of game for another. Wisconsin and Iowa developed such an agreement in the mid-1980s. Wisconsin swapped live-trapped ruffed grouse with Iowa for a supply of that state's wild pheasants.

THE VALUE OF CONSERVATION

Many states in the farm belt are currently striving to find a niche for pheasants in today's farming strategies. It may be too early to draw any definite conclusions, but there is hope that conservationists, farmers, and politicians are beginning to understand that a healthy environment is as valuable as any commodity that can be reaped from the land. It is, quite simply, good business.

George Bush promised "no net loss of wetlands" during his 1988 presidential campaign. The mere fact that a would-be president would refer to a marshland as a "wetland" and not a "swamp" or, worse yet, "worthless swamp" is, we can only hope, a positive change in what was once a common belief. Though Bush failed to deliver on his promise, his language marked a noticeable change in politics. Until recently, most politicians and businessmen saw wetlands as impediments, standing in the way of development, jobs and, ultimately, progress as defined by their own narrow views.

After decades of education, there seems to be a broader understanding of the role of wetlands. Aside from pheasant habitat, wetlands are the reservoirs of the land. Developers scratch their heads as they watch lowland housing projects wash downriver every few years in what is often called a "one-hundred-year" flood. Although steadfast ignoramuses will never believe it, when wetlands are drained, there is no place for storm or melt water to go except down swollen rivers. Wetlands are the sponges that absorb the excess water on the land. Without them floods will continue to destroy property and claim lives with increasing frequency.

Wetland conservation is wise business for other reasons, too. Wetlands filter water and help keep soil on the land. Soil, it can be argued, is America's most valuable natural resource. That fact became particularly apparent throughout the Dust Bowl during what was subsequently called the "Dirty Thirties." A call for soil conservation in the farm belt came on the heels of that great natural disaster. In 1945,

This dated photograph from the Wisconsin Conservation Department—forerunner of the state's Department of Natural Resources—depicts early research conducted on ringnecks at the state's game farm facility near Poynette. (Photo courtesy Wisconsin DNR)

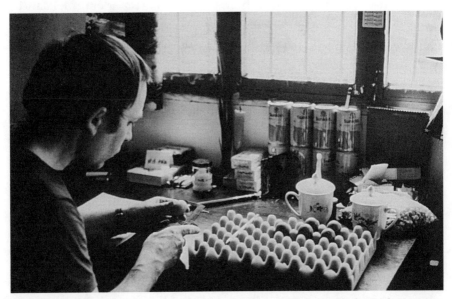

Prior to shipping them to Michigan, this biologist measures the size of Sichuan pheasant eggs collected in China as part of a program to bring the birds stateside. (Photo © by Pete Squibb)

biologist Paul L. Errington advised, "It is imperative that our soils be conserved and even modest incidental gains (for game management) should be wholly acceptable."

All this is to say nothing of the value wetlands have for the wild community. They are havens for a multitude of both game and nongame wildlife, and serve as resting sites for migratory birds as well as year-round habitat for local fauna. It is equally difficult to place a monetary value on wetlands as places where people can relieve their city-born anxieties. Indeed, we are only beginning to appreciate the therapeutic value of wild places such as wetlands.

Wise soil use, too, is often sound wildlife management. The twain are inseparable. While scientific research was needed to conclude much about the life of ringnecks, it was plainly evident that legislated multiyear farmland set-asides were having miraculous effects on pheasant populations.

MODERN RESEARCH

By 1950, what was previously subjective research analysis evolved into a scientific approach to wildlife research. Some of the research that is still considered valid today began to tackle specific questions facing ringneck survival in America. Many popular notions about pheasant management began to tumble under the weight of careful scrutiny. Biologist Durward Allen concluded in his book *Pheasants in North America* that feeding pheasants in winter—which at that time was seen as a wise practice—was neither practical nor economical.

Moreover, a Michigan biologist developed the notion in 1952 that it is nearly impossible to kill too many rooster pheasants in a given population for this reason: As numbers of available cock pheasants dwindle late in a hunting season, hunters enjoy less success and thus hunting becomes self-limiting. When pheasant hunting no longer produces enough birds in the hand, hunters cease to go. This was something of a management epiphany, contradicting the belief that hunters were shooting too many birds. Seasons and bag limits, subsequently, became much more liberal.

As researcher Dr. George Burger noted, "The last foundations had now been pulled from beneath old concepts of the need for refuges and spring releases of cocks, for short hunting seasons, and for closed seasons in years of low populations."

More recent research has caused biologists to rethink previous studies. For example, a 1952 research project concluded that predators—especially red fox—were not a serious threat to pheasant populations. In that era of abundant habitat, D. A. Arnold's conclusion may have been a correct one. More recently, though, retired Wisconsin farmland wildlife specialist Ed Frank suggested to me that today's increasingly small islands of cover may be subject to intensified predation. A fox, for instance, doesn't have to wander unlimited acres of cover in order to find an available meal. Winter landscape throughout much of our best pheasant range is generally composed of a few isolated thickets where virtually all of an area's birds can be found.

A Wisconsin study conducted at the state's Waterloo Wildlife Area in the early 1970s supported this belief. The research indicated that predation was having considerable impact on pheasant populations on the property. Biologists radio-tagged birds to follow them through their lives, tabulated how many survived and, of the ones that died, determined which deaths were due to predation.

More studies in the 1970s continued to blame intensified agriculture and what that brought—wetland drainage, the removal of fencelines, and increased pesticide use—for the demise of the ringneck. Although agriculture was largely responsible for the pheasant boom of the 1940s and 1950s, by the late 1970s and early 1980s many hunters and wildlife biologists were beginning to write the pheasant's obituary.

Modern pheasant hunting in America is the product of a generation of research, habitat management, and continuing land use changes. It's clear that future federal farm legislation will hold the key to pheasant hunting in the twenty-first century.

These South Dakota hunters enjoyed a mixed bag of pheasants and prairie chickens during a hunt about the time World War II came to a close. Note the popularity of the Winchester Model 12 pump guns. (Photo courtesy South Dakota State Historical Society)

This group of Salem, South Dakota, pheasant hunters had a productive day on the prairies. This vintage 1926 photo provides a glimpse into the halcyon years of American pheasant hunting. (Photo courtesy South Dakota State Historical Society)

Exacerbating the problem, funding for pheasant research in most states declined proportionately with pheasant populations—ironically, funding decreases came at a time when information gleaned from more research may have helped stem the downward slide. Furthermore, the destruction of wildlife habitat, and the lack of opportunity to alter that trend, led conservationists to begin managing the remaining pheasant cover along rural roadsides in an almost desperate attempt to bolster wildlife numbers during the early 1980s.

A NEW AGE

As we look to the twenty-first century, pheasants have mounted a resurgence on the heels of the Conservation Reserve Program. New federal laws have also severely restricted wetland drainage, in some cases even mandating that new marshlands be created to offset the previous loss of wetlands.

At no time in recent history have pheasant hunters had as much cause for optimism. As conservationists have learned through years of trial and error, however, implementing conservation measures is a matter of developing a compromise among all users of the land. The degree of cooperation among the farmer, the hunter, and the developer will forever dictate the success of farmland conservation measures.

The Pheasant and the Plow

"THE FAILURE OF WILDLIFE PROFESSIONALS AND ADMINISTRATORS
TO BATTLE, BY EVERY MEANS AVAILABLE, TO INFLUENCE THE
COURSE OF FEDERAL CROPLAND RETIREMENT PROGRAMS MUST BE
VIEWED AS ONE OF CONSERVATION'S GREATEST FAILURES."
—GEORGE BURGER, "100 YEARS OF RINGNECKS"

The Pheasant and the Plow
Sixty Years of Farm Programs

Before there were sixteen-bottom plows and machines big enough to pull them, and before rows of corn stretched all the way to the horizon, there was the small, family farm. This was a time when farms were diversified, raising a mixture of crops as well as beef, dairy cattle, pigs, and poultry. It took an assortment of crops to feed those animals, and farmers went about tending small fields of hay, wheat, corn, and oats.

Pheasants thrived in the small farm habitats. Today, however, when the farmer makes hay, the pheasant doesn't. Modern farms are often mega-monocultures. Diesel is the only food required to feed the beasts that power today's agribusiness machine. While huge fields of alfalfa appear likely nesting cover for pheasants, in reality they are forbidden fruits of sorts, luring pheasants to nest, only to have mowers turn them into mulch. The fast-growing legume is often cut before a hen pheasant can finish incubating her eggs.

In a 1982 report, South Dakota biologist Carl Trautman compared the yearly acreage of alfalfa in that state with the corresponding pheasant harvest. In 1945, the year in which the greatest number of pheasants were taken by hunters, only 2.3 percent of the state's farmland was planted with alfalfa. By 1975, the year with the lowest pheasant harvest, the percentage of alfalfa acreage per farm had risen to 15 percent. In important dairy states

This has become a more common sight throughout much of America's heartland, thanks to the efforts of far-sighted conservationists who lobbied for conservation measures in recent federal farm legislation. (Photo © by Mark Kayser, South Dakota Tourism)

like Wisconsin, alfalfa mowing has also had a negative impact on that state's pheasant populations.

Moreover, the small plots of a bygone era in agriculture created the plentiful edges of cover so often favored by pheasants. Such places offer food and shelter in close proximity. The use of herbicides and insecticides wasn't widespread years ago either. Cropfields were often weedy and home to prolific insects—the same protein-rich bugs that sustain pheasant chicks during the first weeks of their lives.

Scores of such factors have affected pheasants as modern agriculture continues to evolve; wetland drainage, loss of shelterbelts, mowing of roadsides, aerial spraying, and the like all play a role in pheasant survival. To understand the part the federal government has played in agriculture and the success or failure of pheasant management programs, here's a review of major American farm legislation.

HUMBLE BEGINNINGS

The era of such legislation began in 1934, when Congress passed the Cropland Adjustment Act. Under this program, some thirty-seven million acres of farmland were retired, with nearly 80 percent being in twelve midwestern states. Unlike the more recent Conservation Reserve Program, farmers were not required to plant any cover crops, and wildlife management was still largely developing only in ecologist Aldo Leopold's mind. Little was known at the time what effect this program had on farmland wildlife species like the pheasant.

The same was true for the Agriculture Conservation Program (ACP) that lasted from 1936 to 1942. An average of twenty-two million acres of land were retired each year of the program. Unlike its predecessor, however, under ACP farmers had to plant legumes or grasses to meet the provisions of the program. It wasn't until 1984 that biologist W. R. Edwards compared pheasant harvests in the states where ACP was active and showed that pheasant harvests were correspondingly high during the years the program lasted. When the ACP ceased in 1942, moreover, the pheasant bag declined proportionately to the loss of habitat—further reinforcing the belief that the program provided pheasants with sorely needed habitat.

SOIL BANK SUCCESS

The decline in pheasant numbers continued following the end of the ACP, reaching an ebb in 1947. The pheasant population, though, leveled off by the 1950s, and the famous Soil Bank program was implemented in 1956 to conserve soil at a time when we were producing more grain than the market could use.

By 1960, nearly thirty million acres of land had been retired under the Conservation Reserve portion of what was generally referred to as the Soil Bank. Trautman discovered that, in a four year span between 1958 and 1962, nearly 20 percent of pheasant production came from Conservation Reserve lands—this despite the fact that these lands comprised less than 7 percent of the available nesting cover in his South Dakota study area.

During the mid-1960s, studies in Michigan and Utah further documented the beneficial effects of the Soil Bank on pheasant populations. The Soil Bank, not surprisingly, was primarily implemented in the main agricultural states of the Midwest, where pheasant populations were also strongest.

What was the financial impact of these bountiful pheasant populations on states such as South Dakota? In biologist Alfred Berner's analysis of farm programs and their effect on wildlife, he cites economic research conducted by Erickson and Wiebe which "found that numbers of nonresident pheasant hunters were directly correlated to the abundance of South Dakota's pheasants.

"Higher pheasant numbers in the late 1950s and early 1960s, due to improved habitat provided by [the Soil Bank's] Conservation Reserve, resulted in an annual influx of about 50,000 additional nonresident hunters during those years. Conservatively, these additional hunters contributed over $10 million each year to South Dakota's economy. These increased revenues totaled more than 55 percent of the amount spent annually by the federal government to sustain the Conservation Reserve in South Dakota."

A STEP BACKWARD

The USDA's Emergency Feed Grain Program (FGP) of 1961, and another similar program, however, did little to benefit farmland wildlife. The goal of FGP was to increase farmers' incomes by controlling feed grain production through annual set-asides—typically planted to barley, sorghum, corn, and oats. But cover planted under the auspices of this program was often disturbed by early cutting before pheasants could successfully hatch a clutch of eggs.

In 1966, though, biologists were optimistic about a new federal initiative called the Cropland Adjustment Program (CAP) which sported the beneficial features of the Soil Bank—including cropland set-asides, habitat improvement projects, and wetland preservation—as well as financial incentives to landowners to allow hunting on their property. Other programs, unfortunately, had more appeal to farmers than did the CAP, thus leading to its quick demise.

Federal cost-share programs, unlike CAP, have existed since Congress passed the Soil Conservation and Domestic Allotment Act of 1936. Marshlands were drained for over thirty years thanks to cost-share funding provided by the American taxpayer and brought to you by the federal government. According to USDA figures, cost-share funds contributed to the draining of over fifty-two million acres of wetlands! The largest "beneficiaries" of this drainage included Minnesota (4.7 million acres drained), Michigan (3.9 million acres), Missouri (2.9 million acres), and Iowa (2.5 million acres). From 1936 to 1983, USDA spent over $18 billion to garner the "benefits" of fewer wetlands.

Given the well known value of these environs to pheasants and scores of other wildlife species, the cost-share drainage program stands as one of the largest federal programs to negatively impact wildlife in American history. The loss of these critical wetlands has particularly contributed to record low duck numbers across the continent.

THE NEW CONSERVATION RESERVE PROGRAM
The bitter irony of federal money being spent on the wholesale destruction of ecosystems eventually led environmental and conservation groups to lobby Congress for sweeping changes in the

Pheasants and a lone sharptail are able to find bits of grain on this South Dakota silage mound. Exposed piles of seed, spilled grain, and standing crops can often mean the difference between life and death for birds facing severe winters. (Photo © by Ron Spomer)

American pheasant populations can be directly linked to major farm programs. While some programs have been disastrous for farmland wildlife, other programs like the Soil Bank and Conservation Reserve have been enormously beneficial by providing increased habitat. (Photo © by Bob Queen, Wisconsin DNR)

1985 Farm Bill. According to Minnesota biologist Alfred Berner: "These efforts produced federal farm legislation with the strongest conservation provisions written since 1934."

When then President Reagan signed the 1985 Farm Act, or more correctly the 1985 Food Security Act, he activated a program that incorporated six major conservation programs that are still in existence today: Conservation Reserve, Acreage Reduction, Sodbuster, Conservation Compliance, Swampbuster, and Conservation Easements. Of the six facets of the program, most biologists concur that the Conservation Reserve component was the most beneficial to wildlife because it created the most upland habitat.

The 1985 Farm Act differs from other earlier programs in that it is more comprehensive, ". . . linking the stewardship of land, water, and wild living resources with landowner and land operator eligibility for federal farm benefits," according to Laurence Jahn of the Wildlife Management Institute, one of the organizations involved in developing the 1985 Farm Bill.

The Conservation Reserve Program reduces soil erosion by retiring highly erodible land—property on which cover crops or trees must be planted under provisions of the program. According to Jahn's report, CRP has the potential to save more than 610 million tons of topsoil each year, reducing average erosion rates from twenty-two tons per acre per year to 1.7 tons. A natural spin-off benefit of decreased soil erosion is improved water quality. Siltation is a major threat to many river systems and sediment—often laced with chemical fertilizers and pesticides from agricultural runoff—can effectively choke entire bodies of water, killing fish and sport angling along with it.

Although the Acreage Reduction Program offers few soil, water, and wildlife benefits, the Sodbuster provision serves as something of a penalty component whereby no federal farm assistance would be paid to farmers who plowed previously untilled land after 1985 without an approved conservation plan. Sodbuster gets its name because it was designed to discourage farmers from tilling additional soil. Conservation Compliance, meanwhile, withholds federal payments to any farmer who fails to develop a conservation plan for highly erodible land already in crop production.

Under provisions of the next feature, the Swampbuster, the 1985 Farm Bill ended decades of federal policy that often encouraged wetland drainage. Swampbuster targets some seventy million acres of privately owned wetlands. Like Conservation Compliance, Swampbuster denies any federal farm benefits to growers who drain marshlands for the purpose of farming them.

The last provision of the act includes Conservation Easements. This part of the act was administered by the Farmers Home Administration and allowed farmers in financial trouble to rid themselves of a portion of their back taxes in exchange for conservation easements lasting a minimum of fifty years. The acres sought in the easements were often marginal farmland, thus farmers were often receptive to the idea of trading back-debt for rights to a swamp or other "unproductive" lands.

The tales of farm programs and pheasants in America are intertwined. The lessons of the past have shown us that short-term set-asides do little for wildlife, particularly pheasants. Long-term land retirements, however, have proven to be a boon for ringnecks. The foresight and initiative shown by conservationists as the 1985 Farm Bill was being drafted are a testament that perhaps we have learned from the past. Agriculture and wildlife can cohabit, and there is value to a sound environment. And perhaps the people who recognize this are our greatest resource of all.

The Pheasant or the Egg

"HABITAT MANAGEMENT NOTWITHSTANDING, IT APPEARS NOW
THAT THE FIRST CONCERN IS NOT SO MUCH A MATTER OF
CREATING COVER AS OF PREVENTING ITS DESTRUCTION."
—R. A. McCABE

The Pheasant or the Egg
A Year in the Life of the North American Ringneck

While many hunters follow closely the affairs of the ringneck when the rooster becomes a target sometime in October or November, it is the rest of the year that often determines how the drama of the hunt will be performed. Hunters should be, I think, more than the ones to carry a gun. They should, and must, be the voice of the pheasants, the translator of the birds' needs to the rest of society. Without an understanding of those needs, however, there can be no voice.

If hunting is to continue as a sport, it demands that we continually educate the nonhunting public. Recognition of that reality is growing—albeit slowly—among our members. Hunting seasons are all too brief, but the season of the pheasant will last only as long as we allow it, for in our view and comprehension of ecology rests the fate of all things wild.

THE RINGNECK

To look at a hen and a cock pheasant is to seemingly look at two different species. The mottled brown of the hen stands in drab contrast to the brilliantly colored rooster. The cock pheasant looks the way a chicken would if you were to dip the bird in a box of melted crayons. A chickenlike beak protrudes from the rooster's head, on which a fleshy red patch surrounds the bird's eyes. Feathery ear tufts give the cock the appearance of having two small horns. Iridescent green feathers cover the neck until, at its base, a white collar rings it—hence the name "ring-necked" pheasant.

Pheasants will often inhabit the edges of forest and grassland, sometimes seeking shelter there during the hunting season in order to escape the wrath of hunters in the marshes and grasslands. (Photo © by Chris Dorsey)

The large breast of the rooster is protected by feathers ranging in color from black to red to orange to yellow—representing every shade in a picturesque sunset. The back feathers of the cock are almond-colored and lined neatly in a row like fallen dominos. A handful of long brown feathers—usually measuring eighteen to twenty-three inches in an adult bird—sprout from the cock's tail. Thin black lines cross these feathers like the rules on a yardstick.

The rooster, once flushed from cover, often emits a series of throaty crowing or cackling noises. The male also weighs, on average, from 2½ to 3½ pounds. The slightly smaller hen typically ranges from two to three pounds.

Aside from the difference in size, the hen is similar to the rooster in body form but sports a shorter tail and lacks the rooster's colorful plumage. The hen's feathers range from dark brown on its back to an almost cream-colored underbelly. Such coloration serves the hen well by helping to conceal it while nesting in grassy hedgerows and fields.

SPRING

Spring to a pheasant community—for all practical purposes—actually begins in late winter. Cock pheasants initiate the struggle for dominance, participating in a tournament where the winners will earn the right to collect a harem of hens. As spring nears, the winter flocks disband, and roosters seek turf of their own in which to begin crowing their eligibility to receptive females. While most roosters remain near their winter haunts, a South Dakota study documented a case where one bird journeyed over ten miles to establish his territory. Fighting intensity and crowing frequency increase the closer the birds come to the peak of the breeding season.

A pheasant population's breeding season will vary depending upon what part of the species' North American range it is in. The season may begin as early as late March in the southern range and as late at early June in the north.

Hunters—especially those who fancy themselves armchair biologists—often fret over the loss of too many roosters during the hunting seasons. "There aren't enough roosters to breed the hens," they proclaim. "We ought to close the season for a year or two." While their intentions are admirable, research has continually shown that even a small number of roosters in a pheasant population is capable of servicing virtually all available hens. In one study, for instance, a wild cock pheasant was known to have bred twenty hens in his harem. Another experiment gave a rooster sole dominion over fifty hens in a penned enclosure. Biologists' examinations of the resulting eggs from the hens revealed nearly 90 percent of them were fertile. A rooster in the wild, however, will most likely have but three or four hens in his flock.

Hens seldom have to be bred more than once in order to remain fertile over the initial egg-laying period. One breeding will ensure fertile eggs for an average of three weeks, or about twenty-one days. Since hens lay only one egg every one or two days during the laying period, and because clutch sizes range from eight to twelve eggs during the first nesting attempt, three weeks is usually ample time in which to produce a fertile clutch of pheasant eggs. Only after the clutch is completed does the hen begin incubating her eggs, thus ensuring near-synchronous hatching of all the eggs.

May is for maternity in pheasantdom. Depending upon the length of daylight, the peak of the nesting period normally occurs this month throughout most of the birds' range. Weather also plays a crucial role in nesting success and, subsequently, in the numbers of pheasants available for harvest in the fall. If it's too cold, the eggs may freeze. Too warm and they may addle. Indeed, when one considers the scores of factors working against pheasants—weather, predators, agriculture, and the lack of cover—it seems nothing short of a miracle that any birds survive at all.

Most pheasants, in fact, do not survive. Birthdays for pheasants—like anniversaries for newlyweds—are celebrated in months, not years. Despite the diligent efforts of the hen to protect her chicks for the first two months of their lives, one-quarter of her offspring will die before they are even two weeks old. Half of the brood will likely be lost shortly after their two month birthday.

The spring nesting season can be especially trying for hen pheasants—particularly if it is prolonged. Laying a clutch of eggs drains the hen of many essential minerals, including calcium. Hens will seek out snails and grit for the sole purpose of replenishing the calcium lost during eggshell production. Hen mortality during exceptionally long nesting seasons may actually be heavier than that experienced during the bitter months of winter.

A hen's nesting season will be prolonged if her clutch is

The brightly colored rooster is remarkably adept at concealing itself in dense cover. The fleshy red eye patch of a rooster becomes engorged with blood during the spring mating season and is set-off by the white feather necklace. (Photo © by Chris Dorsey)

destroyed by a nest predator such as a raccoon, fox, or skunk. If she loses her clutch, she will usually renest. If the nest was destroyed while the hen was still laying and had not completed her clutch, renesting usually occurs within a day or two after the hen's eggs are lost. If the hen had already completed her clutch and was incubating, she may not begin her new nest for two to four days. Renesting usually occurs relatively near the destroyed nest. The new clutch, however, will contain fewer eggs than the hen produced, or would have produced, in her first nesting attempt. Should a hen lose her second clutch to a predator, she may go on to renest yet again.

When the chicks hatch—following twenty-three days of incubation—they are covered in a fuzzy down. The chicks are termed "precocial" because of their ability to move and catch their own food in the form of insects shortly after hatching. As soon as the chicks have hatched and their down has dried, the hen leads them from the nest in search of seeds and insects. The yolk sacks that sustained the birds throughout their development inside the egg are nearly exhausted by now, and the chicks are hungry.

Random spraying of insecticides at this time of year can be especially detrimental to chick survival, for it is insects that comprise the staple of a chick's diet. For the first month following the hatch, the family unit will likely remain within a ten-acre area. The birds aren't known to be far ranging, normally living their entire lives within a two-square-mile area.

SUMMER

Young pheasants don't remain grounded for long. Chicks can make short-leap flights within two weeks of hatching as their primary wing feathers have already begun developing. This was a fact painfully apparent to me when I first raised a clutch of pheasants in my garage many years ago. After I spent three weeks diligently

Though called albino by many hunters, this color-variation ringneck is rare in the wilds. A true albino is even more rare. (Photo © by Chris Dorsey)

Heavy snows, driving winds, and bitter cold all combine to take their toll on pheasant populations. Sheltering winter cover is an important component of any sustainable pheasant flock's habitat. (Photo © by Mark Kayser, South Dakota Tourism)

turning the pheasant eggs in my incubator, the first birds began to peck circles in the tops of their egg shells. A twenty-inch-high wall of hardware cloth around a bed of newspapers served as the initial home for the hatchlings.

The birds developed nicely in the topless cage until one morning when I stepped out of the house to feed them only to find half the birds running willy-nilly through the garage. Though their bumble bee bodies remained wrapped in down, their juvenile primary feathers allowed their wings to propel them from the cage and to the liberty of my cluttered garage. Catching these liberated birds was a family affair; unfortunately it occurred before the days of home video cameras when the hilarity of the moment could have been captured.

Had these birds been born in the wild, they would have moved from their nesting environs to what is referred to as brood-rearing cover. There is no line drawn in the field dividing nesting cover from brood-rearing cover. There is a great deal of overlap, with pheasants using a variety of cover throughout the year. Brood-rearing cover is essentially an extension of nesting cover. Biologists simply type different kinds of cover based on the frequency of seasonal use by pheasants. Cover commonly frequented in winter, not surprisingly, is termed winter cover. Pheasants aren't bothered by such classifications; they only know that such cover keeps the wind and snow from their feathers and the hawks from snatching them from above.

By the time pheasants are two months old, they are completely feathered. This is their juvenile plumage, however, and it is still impossible to distinguish hens from roosters by feathering since they both wear the same brown coat. By the time they are nine weeks old, pheasants enter their post-juvenile molt. Then the brilliant red feathers of the roosters sprout one-by-one on their chests, replacing the juvenile feathers, the same way a ptarmigan

Having survived the winter, this South Dakota rooster prepares for the spring breeding season in which he will actively court a harem of hens. (Photo © by Mark Kayser, South Dakota Tourism)

After crops have been harvested from the field, predators like this coyote concentrate their hunting efforts in the islands of cover that remain on the land. The less habitat, the easier the hunting. (Photo © by Herb Lange)

Though red fox feed predominantly on small rodents, they will, on occasion, take pheasants. Heavy predation seldom occurs, however, in areas where pheasants are afforded ample escape cover. (Photo © by Herb Lange)

Raccoons and skunks are nest raiders, though they will eat a variety of plant and animal life. A hen pheasant will commonly renest if her first nest is destroyed, but subsequent nests are seldom as large as the first clutch. (Photo © by Herb Lange)

loses its white coat of winter, feather-by-feather.

FALL

Sometime between their fourth and fifth month birthday, the birds will be nearly indistinguishable from their adult counterparts. Life remains relatively easy for the pheasant at this time as food and cover are normally abundant. Pheasants are omnivorous and their adaptability to many types of cover and food is largely responsible for their success on this continent. Cropfields provide the birds with both food and cover—effectively allowing them to remain protected throughout the day. Cornfields are particular favorites of fall pheasants, providing an overhead canopy while offering a clear understory where the birds are free to move about, secure from avian predators.

Such areas—called loafing sites in biological vernacular—are important throughout the year. In spring, loafing cover may be a young stand of willows bordering a wetland. In winter, a wooded ravine might also provide loafing cover among a mixture of hardwoods and evergreens.

Hunters know this and explore the many lairs of the pheasant during the hunting season. Fall is an especially challenging time for pheasants. As combines chew off the crops, they take with them the roof and walls of the places pheasants call home. Until then, the farm fields provided the birds food and cover, but like life itself, the crops are taken from them without warning.

Pheasants are forced to adjust to their shrinking environs or perish. Those that heed lessons well, or those that are lucky, will survive running the gauntlet of fall. The rest will be served over toast or eaten hastily as fox fodder. Those are the unwavering realities of life in the wild. Nature is undaunted by her loss.

WINTER

Winter is the ultimate test for most species of wildlife; the pheasant is no exception. It is something of a bitter irony for the pheasant: When it needs the protection of cover most, there is the least amount of it on the land. When arctic winds blow across the plains and the landscape is flooded in a sea of frozen snow, pheasants eke out an existence on the few weed seeds and kernels of grain that may yet be on the land. Deep snows, however, bury any spilled grain that wasn't already turned under by the plow. One can't help but admire the wherewithal of a pheasant that manages to defy the incredible odds and survive such perils.

Pheasants, though, are robust birds. They are able to withstand long periods of bitter cold, but don't fare as well under the stresses brought about by a blizzard. In his report, *History, Ecology and Management of the Ring-necked Pheasant in South Dakota,* Carl Trautman cites a 1967 study in which a three-day blizzard in 1966 killed 86 percent of the pheasant population in several of the state's north-central counties.

The birds that survive the initial blast of a blizzard must still cope with the remaining heavy snow. Such snows force birds into the protective cover of woody environs, often further from sources of food. The birds must then travel longer distances from cover in order to eat, thus becoming more susceptible to predation.

A wet spring coupled with early winter snowfalls, however, can provide something of a life raft for pheasants waiting for the rescue of spring to melt its way to them. Farmers are unable to comb some sodden cornfields with heavy combines when early snows saturate the land, and standing corn often remains in the fields until spring. In the interim, the pheasant collects interest on the intrusion into its domain, kernel by kernel.

The misfortune of the farmer is a boon for the pheasant. Though some of my best friends are farmers, I register a silent cheer

Pheasants can also fall prey to great horned owls as well as several species of hawks. Such avian predation occurs chiefly along woody edges or woodlands where the raptors are able to survey surrounding landscapes from elevated perches. (Photo © by Herb Lange)

Roosters begin crowing in late winter to establish their breeding territories. In the process of attracting hens to his territory, however, the cock pheasant becomes especially vulnerable to predators. (Photo © by Ron Spomer)

Pheasant chicks are precocial, able to walk and find food shortly after hatching. Insects comprise much of a chick's diet for the first several weeks of its life. (Photo courtesy Wisconsin DNR)

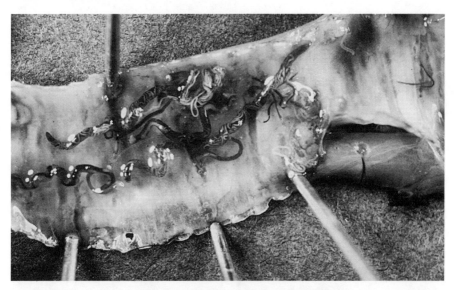

Here biologists examine a gapeworm infestation in the trachea of a pheasant as part of ongoing research at the U.S. Fish & Wildlife Service's National Wildlife Health Lab. Funding for such research is critical if healthy pheasant populations are to continue. (Photo © by Milt Friend, National Wildlife Health Lab)

at the sight of such fields captured by the sudden advances of winter. They give me hope that there will be birds there next year and places to fill my game bag with memories.

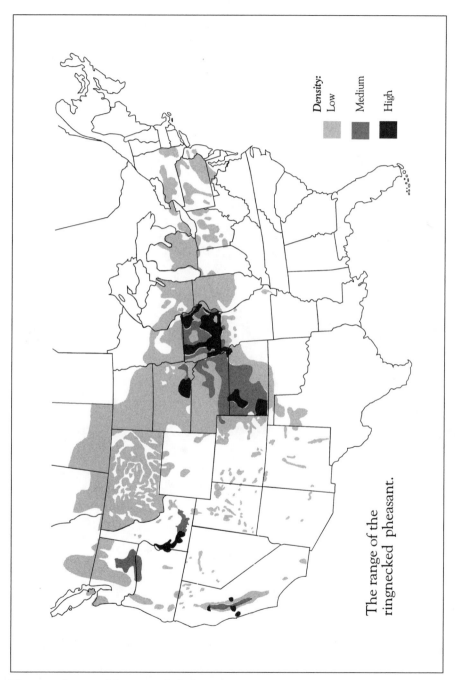

The general range of the ringnecked pheasant.

Two Sides to the Same Bird

"THE GOOD NEWS IS THAT THERE ARE PROBABLY GOING TO BE
MORE OF THESE BIRDS [PHEASANTS] THAN THERE HAVE BEEN FOR A
NUMBER OF YEARS; THE BAD NEWS IS THEY'RE GOING TO BE JUST AS
HARD TO GET IN THE AIR AND KILL AS THEY ALWAYS WERE."
—*STEVE SMITH*, HUNTING UPLAND GAME BIRDS

Two Sides to the Same Bird
Early Birds
or Better Late than Ever

EARLY SEASON

I'll never forget my first opening day on a public hunting area some fifteen years ago. I made the drive to Mud Lake Wildlife Area to partake in the noon opener of Wisconsin's pheasant season. A narrow road ran through the middle of the property and served as the area's only access. When I arrived—about 11:45 A.M.—the road was choked with parked cars, pickups, and vans. At least a hundred hunters and their dogs waited along the shoulder of the road, each with expectations of finding one of the pen-raised roosters the state released here only the week before.

I couldn't help but notice the many fathers and their young sons and a few daughters—for many it may have been their first exposure to pheasant hunting or, perhaps, even to hunting in general. It was far different than the quiet hike my brother and I made behind our old farmhouse in search of roosters when I was twelve. There is something fitting about sharing a first hunt with someone close to you, learning the way of the hunter from someone whom you respect and admire. There was no sense of confusion brought about by too many hunters in too small an area. Nor was there a sense of competition, only a general reverence for the bird and the moment.

My quiet, homegrown hunt was a stark contrast to the masses huddled at roadside, awaiting the noon whistle to signal the opening of the pheasant season as though it were kickoff at a football stadium. It was, regrettably, a symptom of the era. There are ever-shrinking opportunities to garner access to land that might hold pheasants. For many hunters, then, public hunting areas offer the only viable option in a place to hunt.

Shortly after noon, rows of hunters entered the public land, combing the cover for birds. About mid-way through, cocks began to flush and the reports of shotgun blasts could be heard all the way to the woods where I sat with my setter, Thor, waiting for the escaping birds to cross our path.

It wasn't long before a rooster managed to avoid the barrage below in the grass and alighted nearby in the woods. Thor saw the bird land some forty yards away, and the setter quickly quartered into the wind until he found the bird hidden under the brush of a fallen oak. I took the bird with the second shot as it cleared a stand of sumac. Though I haven't spent an opening day on that property for years, I imagine that it is as popular as ever.

I now make a special effort before the season to visit landowners who have let me hunt their property during previous seasons, reaffirming my appreciation for the privilege. These places are more valuable to me now than they have ever been. With each passing year, I have more memories invested in each haunt. It pains me, though, to drive country roads that lead past retired covers.

A marsh I once traveled with setter and pump shotgun during my college years is now a sod farm. Where once there were cattails aplenty and all the wildlife that they brought—ducks, geese, herons, swans, muskrats, songbirds, and the like—there is now a flat carpet of four-inch sod surrounded by a moat of water channeled from the land. To blame the farmer for selling out would simply be selfish. I didn't pay him to hunt on the land, I should be grateful that he let me hunt his property as long as he did. Still, there is a natural sense of anger that I feel compelled to direct toward someone.

Pheasant calls like this one made by Olt can be used to locate and even lure roosters to land in your vicinity. The "plastic pooch," as author C. M. Petrie calls it, is an ideal way to take roosters when you don't have the services of a dog. (Photo © by Chuck Petrie)

Walking and pausing in likely pheasant cover is a good way to induce roosters like this to flush. The idea is to make pheasants nervous by making them guess where you are when you stop abruptly in the field. Such a tactic is a particularly good way to hunt if you're alone and without a dog. (Photo © by Mark Kayser, South Dakota Tourism)

Pheasants are amazing runners. One minute you may see them and the next minute they may be two hundred yards away—without having taken wing. (Photo © by Mark Kayser, South Dakota Tourism)

In practical terms, the only way to hedge against losing your favorite hunting hideouts—short of buying a section of land—is to continually recruit new areas. A month or two before the season is a good time to begin your search. While it can often be hot throughout much of the pheasant's North American range in August and early September, the hour before sunset often offers temperatures cool enough to work your dog without fear of it suffering from heat stress.

Few landowners will object to you simply running your dog in their meadows or marshlands. If your jaunt produces birds, you'll want to seek permission to hunt on the land come October or November. This method allows you to both condition your dog for upcoming hunting work as well as locate new hunting grounds. The best dog and tactics pale beside the benefits of having access to great pheasant habitat.

Much of the most productive cover throughout the pheasant's

range is found near cropfields such as corn. Pheasant hunters come to develop a love-hate relationship with cornfields. While standing corn helps sustain pheasant populations, it is difficult cover in which to hunt birds. Typically, pheasants simply sprint out of shotgun range—usually without the hunter even knowing of the bird's presence.

For the first few weeks of the season, however, pheasants will remain in their grassy roosts until the frost and dew have dried from the stems. It is during this morning light that early season hunters have an opportunity to find pheasants before they move to the corn. Hunt the edges where corn and grass meet, but never hunt the grass *toward* a cornfield—you will simply drive the pheasants to the safety of the corn without them ever having to expose themselves to your wrath by taking wing. The idea, of course, is to get between the birds and the standing corn where your dog will be able to locate them within shotgun range.

The last hour of daylight is another good time to find pheasants in the grass. If the birds haven't been hunted heavily, they will often fly from the corn to their favorite nightly roosting sites—commonly cackling while they wing their way in. Find an elevated vantage overlooking a wetland or weed field just prior to dusk. When the birds fly from the cover, mark their landing location and quickly try to flush them before they have a chance to scamper away.

This is also a fine time to entice the birds out of the corn by using a pheasant call. Olt manufactures such a call and is only slightly more difficult to use than a duck call. By hiding in prime roosting cover, a hunter can entice birds out of the corn with a single cackle. It is a peculiar way to hunt pheasants, but can be used successfully given the right conditions.

LATE SEASON

Late season means snow. The world of the pheasant and the

pheasant hunter changes with the first coating of snow on the land. Snow provides observant hunters with an intimate look at the world of the ringneck. Spend a morning after a new snow retracing the steps taken by a ringneck and you will learn much about it: where it seeks shelter; what food is sustaining it through the winter; how it avoids predators; whether it is a hen or a rooster.

It is at this time of year that the hunter without a dog is at no disadvantage vis-à-vis friends who have dogs. A quiet morning walk among frozen cattails and packing snow belies the raucous flush of a rooster that can come at any moment. A rooster track, compared to that made by a hen, is most notable by the difference in gait and size. The seasoned hunter quickly distinguishes the two and concentrates on the rooster track, half again larger than that made by a hen.

Such stalking is rife with excitement. Will the cock be in the next cover of cattails? Has he already flushed? Will the prints lead you to other birds? Read carefully the signs left by the birds and you will soon discover the answers.

A pheasant's life is carefree when his tracks amble and twist through cover, each print in the snow but a hand's width apart. Foxtail seeds might be sprinkled about the snow where the bird paused to peck the furry tip of the plant, spilling many seeds in the process. Faint wing impressions left behind in the snow mark a place where a rooster, content with his affairs, crowed and shuffled his feathers to let others know of his mood.

You can be certain that the bird knows of your presence, however, when the distance between its foot prints widen from about four or five inches to twelve to sixteen inches apart. He is now in escape mode, and has several options available to him—running and flying being two notable choices. Even the best laid plans will not put you on course to shoot experienced roosters. A gun-shy rooster may spook for friendlier surroundings at the first

The cover surrounding abandoned farmsteads is often overlooked by hunters but commonly provides shelter near cropfields—all the ingredients needed to hold birds. (Photo © by Mark Kayser, South Dakota Tourism)

slam of a nearby car door or toot of a dog whistle. Heavily hunted roosters are particularly susceptible to developing such a conditioned response. Such birds provide the genes necessary to ensure that future hunters are frustrated by the same prowess.

There are enough pheasants, thankfully, that do not opt to flush early and come to be known as Thanksgiving dinner for those who are persistent. There are the birds that choose to run to nearby patches of cattail where they mistakenly wait for danger to pass them by. Pheasants, you see, do not understand the concept of tracking.

Therefore, cancel social plans and fabricate an illness in order to get out of work when a few inches of snow have fallen overnight. The new covering of powder effectively erases all previous tracks, making the hunter's job of discerning fresh tracks from old, and a rooster's from a hen's, all the easier. With snow on the ground, a quick study of pheasant movements in the powder can teach a hunter how pheasants might be avoiding you at other times of the year.

Snow can also be used as a training assistant to provide dogs an opportunity to become accustomed to wild birds. By locating cover complete with pheasant tracks, the hunter can be certain that there are birds nearby and won't waste time in unproductive cover. The value to this is that you will know when your dog is near birds, thus you can coax it in the right direction by simply following the tracks. Do not be surprised, however, if your pup shows little interest in following pheasant tracks. A dog may find the bird's nearby body scent far more alluring than mere prints in the snow.

It is this quality time with a pup, and exposure to wild birds, that will turn an impressionable youngster into a seasoned hunter. Dogs that have logged countless hours chasing wild ringnecks develop identifiable approaches to birds.

Perhaps the most notable characteristic of such dogs is the need

This hunter waited at the end of a small cornfield while two other hunters walked the field toward him. The drive produced shooting at this escaping rooster. (Photo © by Chris Dorsey)

The edges of creeks provide excellent places in which to trap roosters between a hunter and the water—forcing the bird to flush in order to make its escape. This Montana hunter has done just that as a rooster launches from the edge of this small stream. (Photo © by Chris Dorsey)

to trap birds between themselves and their owners. This is accomplished when the dog deliberately loops around birds to pin them between itself and the gunner. Such a tactic paralyzes roosters. They are uncertain from where the greatest danger is coming and, confused, are more apt to simply remain still in the grass. While pen-raised birds provide aspiring bird dogs with an introduction to game, only wild pheasants can provide the graduate studies necessary to complete a bird dog's education.

Pheasant hunting is, as much as anything, a learning experience. For the hunter and dog who heed lessons well, there will always be birds ahead, for as author Steve Grooms wrote, "Pheasant hunting is a thinking man's game, more arcane and complicated than chess."

Pheasant Hunting
Across America

"... THIS COCKY, SUBTLE, COURAGEOUS, AND EXTRAVAGANTLY
BEAUTIFUL BIRD ... MAKES PHEASANT HUNTING THE INTOXICATING,
FRUSTRATING, AND ALTOGETHER WONDERFUL SPORT THAT IT IS."
—STEVE GROOMS, PHEASANT HUNTER'S HARVEST

Pheasant Hunting Across America

Much of the success of the ringneck is due to its remarkable adaptability. In America, it's found from the cane fields of Hawaii to the woodlots of New England. The bird has also become a familiar resident in the wetlands of the Great Lakes and has gained nearly demigod status on the prairie plains.

Wherever it's found, it provides a flush of adrenalin. But in the multitude of environs it inhabits, each hunt offers a unique flavor—seasoned by mountain peaks in the West and marshlands in the East. What follows are the chronicles of four distinctly different hunts, yet they all journey to the same place—pheasant country.

Montana: Pheasants Between the Peaks

A DIFFERENT GAME AWAITS IN THE WEST

Wildlife artists are forever painting scenes of pheasants perched atop fence posts or rusted wagon wheels on the open plains. In Montana—the land of snow-covered peaks and Big Sky—pheasants are found in a dramatically different landscape. Monuments of stone fractured from the earth's crust jut above verdant valleys in a theater made for gods. I had longed to make a trip to Montana to stalk pheasants, and in 1990 I did, even passing up an opportunity to hunt South Dakota—one of America's premier pheasant hunting states. It didn't seem altogether logical, but I couldn't resist the stories of fantastic pheasant hunting among some of the continent's most captivating scenery.

As I walked through that country, the grassland valley that welcomed me was surrounded by picturesque bluffs—the kind that might have been appropriate subjects for an Ansel Adams portrait. They were signs of sorts that said "Welcome to pheasant hunting in the West." The specter of pheasant hunting is enough to put a silly grin on my face, but pheasant hunting in the stunning landscape found in Montana is, well, positively irresistible. I discovered, too, that Montana pheasants have a run–like–a–mother approach to life, which is to say they are indistinguishable from their eastern counterparts.

Joining me on my birding junket was Montanan Ed Gerrity, a kennel operator from Belgrade. Our rendezvous began at a ranch near Ryegate. It is the kind of place where the Marlboro Man might live, or at least the locals dress as if they are auditioning for the part. Hunters here dream of elk, sheep, bear, and mule deer. Few people pay much attention to the Chinese imports that thrive along area river bottoms—the birds crow their presence to a seemingly deaf audience. Hunters here, for the most part, keep eyes and ears turned toward the mountains, overlooking the pheasants under their noses. I was content to let those hunters be distracted by their four-footed quarry. The pheasant, to be sure, was my big game.

We started our Ryegate hunt along a small winding river edged with high grass and cattail. Gerrity's nine-year-old golden retriever had the redeeming quality of finding and flushing pheasants at close range. The whizbang's name was Tai, known locally as The Wonder Dog.

Though Montana is best known for its superb big game hunting and world-class trout streams, it is also home to fabulous pheasant hunting. This hunter was able to track a rooster through snow to eventually flush it along the edge of a cattail slough. (Photo © by Denver Bryan)

I was mesmerized by the surroundings, awed by the adjacent bluffs that climbed from the earth. Before I could finish absorbing the beauty of the scene, however, Tai sent a pair of hens flushing past me. One, two, then three more hens spooked before a lone rooster flew from a dried-up creek bottom. The brightly colored cock seemed almost out of place in a landscape dominated by gray and brown, like a fluorescent crankbait floating across a dark autumn pond.

I cheeked my weathered SKB and intercepted the bird with a load of sixes. In moments, the golden delivered the bird to my grasp. It was an event to be repeated a half dozen times for Ed and me this day. It was also an event that remains as sweet to me now as it was when I first encountered the birds two decades ago on a midwestern farm.

In pheasant hunting there are moments of heightened excitement brought on by feverish dog work, followed by sudden exhilaration when an astonished rooster launches skyward. Tai was one dog that knew the subtle difference between mere cover and *pheasant* cover. It is seemingly a conditioned response—every bit as strong as one induced by Pavlov—bird dogs develop after years of pursuing wild pheasants in their natural habitat. Experienced dogs seek out cover similar to habitat in which they have found birds in the past.

Between pheasant haunts, Gerrity and I cruised the many miles necessary to get from Nowhere to Somewhere, Montana—population: three prairie dogs, two boulders, and a sage hen. Doc Watson picked "Tennessee Stud" on Bozeman's KGLT radio station while Gerrity acquainted me with life under the Big Sky. He is an odd mix of nine-tenths hippie and one-tenth yuppie (that makes him, I think, a yippie). He's a hunter who cherishes Montana's natural wealth and speaks with an almost parental passion about protecting its resources.

The dramatic landscape of Montana is indicative of pheasant hunting theaters across the West. Fertile valleys planted to grains create an inviting atmosphere for both pheasants and pheasant hunters. (Photo © by Denver Bryan)

Gerrity abandoned his native state of Illinois after agribusiness nearly completed the job of flushing its topsoil and wildlife down the Mississippi River. He determined that the same won't happen to Montana. He might have stepped from the pages of an Edward Abbey novel in the form of the muckraking character, Heyduke. Abbey fans slap bumper stickers on their burned-out Volkswagen vans that proclaim "Heyduke Lives." Yes, Heyduke lives, right here in Montana, and he loves to hunt pheasants.

We took our adventure further down Highway 12 and stopped at Lavina, Montana. From that moment we were in the capable hands of Dave and Deb Harmon. Dave is a taxidermist, guide, and family man. Deb may simply be the best damn cook west of the Bearpaws. Dave has spent his entire life in these parts and knows of the blood, sweat, and tears that are a rich part of the community's fabric. Ranchers here know him and trust him. In a state where times are tough, no one can repossess a man's reputation, and it's worth something here.

It was Dave's reputation that allowed Ed and me access to the wealth of pheasant hunting available in the area. Small creek bottoms and lowland fields provided a mixture of meadow and woods that harbored most of the region's birds. Slow flowing switchback creeks roam willy-nilly through the Montana countryside as veins of life. It is here where you will find not only pheasants, but also ducks, whitetails, turkeys, mule deer, and an assortment of predators and furbearers as well. Find water and you will very likely find game. It is an axiom that holds true nearly the world over.

Our pheasant excursions were often abridged so that we could plan a stalk on an unsuspecting flock of mallards that might have alighted in the stream. Such are the virtues of wingshooting in Montana, a state where deer outnumber people. Tai's olfactory magic again guided us to birds. One time I led a cottonwood perfectly on my first shot, hitting the enormous tree as I swung on a rooster along a stream bottom. Gerrity's follow-up shot assured that Tai would get work retrieving the cock as it fell on the other side of the riffling stream.

After departing from the fruitful covers near Lavina, Gerrity and I ambled back to Bozeman, cultural center of the fertile Gallatin Valley. Should we cast some streamers for trout? How 'bout a river goose hunt? Whitetails, anyone? Pheasants, oh yes, they're here, too. Some people complain that there is nothing to do in Montana, others fret that there isn't enough time to do everything.

Gerrity and I were busy trying to disprove the latter. After turning right at a nearby pond that was teeming with waterfowl, we bounced along the gravel road to a nearby farm, the site of the next leg in our pheasant junket across the state.

A weathered, gray barn seemingly teetered on the brink of collapse, perhaps standing as a symbol of the nation's imperiled farm condition. Behind the building grew stunning white peaks

While traipsing the ditches of Montana's Three Cross Ranch near Ryegate, the author was able to take a pair of handsome roosters. The diversity of terrain that the ringneck is now found in is a tribute to its adaptability. (Photo © by Ed Gerrity)

where the region's rivers are born. The canary grass and sedge meadows that grew adjacent to the water were occupied by many creatures, but it was the pheasants that we were most concerned about this day.

Tai's interest in the birds was apparent from the cock of his ears and his eager tail wag that acted as a gauge, measuring the amount of nearby pheasant scent. The look in a bird dog's eyes first gave rise to the term "determination." Over logs and through the river, the golden coursed the valley, drawn to the aroma of pheasants like metal shavings to a magnet. The power of such a hunt is found in its simplicity. It is the kind of power that can charge every electron in your body, stimulate your senses to respond instantaneously to such stimuli as the sound of a flushing pheasant or the feel of cold wind over your face.

It was Tai's body language that continually gave hint of nearby pheasants and prepared me for the subsequent whirlwind of a flushing rooster. I quietly skirted the outer edge of brush that grew adjacent to a meandering stream while watching Ed and Tai course the opposite bank. I was content to watch the pair, both hunters well seasoned in the fine art of pheasant foolery.

Next to the streamside brush were hundreds of acres of newly harvested wheat—fields and skies so golden and blue that not even Kodachrome could capture the vividness. The rugged landscape is alive here, perhaps more so than any other place I have ever been. Hunting is just the excuse I need to journey to Montana. A week is hardly enough time to get to know such a place, but it is possible to walk many memories into your thoughts in Montana. It is, as much as anything, a state where hunters go to live their dreams—a place where fantasy meets reality in forest and field.

Kansas: Corn Belt Pheasants

THE SWEETEST CORN OF ALL

It is easy to dislike hunters in pheasant-rich Kansas. They know nothing of the toils many other pheasant hunters face—like shortages of birds. Theirs is a world where pheasants are vermin, as common as earthworms. I found one such place and it's located a good bit east of Eden, a while past Lake Wobegon, and this side of Shangri-la. It's in a small corner of Kansas that is seemingly only accessible by time travel. You'll know you're there when the pheasants along the roads outnumber the blackbirds in the air.

This place is an anachronism, it belongs to the halcyon years of American pheasant hunting. When you cross into Kearny County, you cross more than a county line. You are transported to a 1961 Soil Bank field—abundant cover gushing with birds—that you thought could only exist in South Dakota. You seem to enter an age when pheasants were as plentiful as fence posts.

LESSONS FROM HISTORY

As the fences were ripped from the land, however, pheasants vanished piecemeal from America's farmland. Iron glaciers called John Deere, Allis Chalmers, and others cultivated the era of high-tech agribusiness, making the land suitable for farming instead of making the farming suitable for the land.

Farmers blanketed the Midwest with cash crops and defended their grain from insects with artillery in the form of discs and plows while continuing a persistent aerial bombardment of deadly organophosphates from under the wings of crop dusters. We proved that America's breadbasket was indeed the world's bread-basket. The question was, for how long?

It wasn't until we exported our technology and subsequently

gave other nations the means to feed themselves that it became apparent that we no longer needed to work the land tirelessly in an effort to meet world demand. The price of our productivity, however, was high. The pesticides sprayed in clouds over cropfields left a sick landscape in the aftermath. Heavy doses of chemical fertilizers, wetland drainage, and fall plowing added to the destruction of the ecosystem. When the impact of the environmental contamination was finally understood—thanks to such works as Rachel Carson's 1962 classic, *Silent Spring*—bureaucrats in Washington took notice.

Over twenty years later, President Reagan signed the historic 1985 Farm Bill. Although chastised by conservationists for his support of controversial Interior Secretary James Watt and a budgetary gutting of the Environmental Protection Agency and Soil Conservation Service, Reagan's signature was attached to one of the most comprehensive farm bills of the century. The impact for hunters and farmers has been dramatic throughout the pheasant's middle America range.

The bill allowed farmers to rest large tracts of their land, which in turn gave farmland wildlife a chance to recover from over two decades of intensive agriculture. Pheasant populations in South Dakota, Nebraska, Iowa, and Kansas have begun a rebound similar to their recovery in the days of the Soil Bank of the 1950s and 1960s.

MODERN IMPROVEMENTS

The beginning of the recovery was apparent to me as I stepped from the Suburban onto my Kansas pheasant field of dreams. There, as far as I could scan, was an endless sea of ripened sorghum lined with ravines like stationary wave troughs reaching across the horizon. It was a place that bird dogs dream of when their paws twitch nervously in their sleep. It was also land in which the pheasant gods could have whispered, "If you plant it, they will

Actor Jameson Parker, co-star of the television series "Simon & Simon," pauses with his seven-year-old Chesapeake Bay retriever during a late-season hunt in Kansas. (Photo© by Chris Dorsey)

come."

The man to answer those pleas was J. R. Dienst, the owner of the thirty thousand acres of heaven upon which we were hunting.

"Should we start here?" I asked.

"This is as good a place as any," said J. R.

He was being modest. The place was covered with bird sign—pheasant tracks littered the place like prints in a well-stocked chicken coop. Of Dienst's thirty thousand acres, roughly five thousand are enrolled in the federal Conservation Reserve Program, perhaps the most beneficial offshoot of the 1985 Farm Bill.

It's funny how hunting can bring so many people from different walks of life together. Our group consisted of Kansas writer Mike Pearce; Bud Ward, a New York publisher; Jameson Parker, an actor between gigs; and Mike Murphy, a fine gun dealer from Wichita.

After injecting our shotguns with loads of six shot, we began a procession across the cover. Bud awaited our arrival at the other end of the sorghum and big bluestem, the recipient of an American-style driven shoot. A hen flushed from the switchgrass in front of Jameson's Chesapeake Bay retriever and soon the gray January sky was punctuated with russet and brown as a flurry of pheasants, each one inciting another to fly, burst from the grassy cover. Such pheasant hunting is pure Pandemonium. Young dogs enter a state of temporary insanity as their owners frantically try to distinguish between the drab hens and the gaudy cocks.

Although a few birds strayed within shooting range, most of the roughly forty pheasants in the flock knew what our presence meant and chose to flush a hundred or more yards ahead of us, escaping to the safe haven of distant cover. While some disdain the confusion that naturally accompanies hunting in groups, it isn't without a charm of its own. I have never hunted with a dog that was worth a lick that didn't—at least on rare occasion—surrender to its wild nature and chase pheasants hither and yon.

I stood as a spectator on the lip of a deep ravine, watching the aftermath of the momentary commotion of pheasant flushes and shotgun barrages. Dogs scampered willy-nilly, the bird scent so strong that it filled their sinus cavities and evidently plugged their ear drums as well. The other hunters shouted and blew whistles at their dogs, mostly adding to the bedlam of the moment. I laughed as only a hunter who had no dogs to be tethered could laugh.

There were dogs in every age group and stage of training, from Murphy's hell-bent-for-birds Lab pup to Pearce's seasoned golden retriever, the would-be sage of the lot. I chuckled at the spectacle because I know the frustrations and joys of raising bird dogs and have been—like every bird dog owner—in the same uncontrollable situation at one time or another. The more infrequent such moments, the easier it is to laugh them off.

"There's a bird down over here."

"Max, fetch . . . fetch!"

"Mysti's got it."

"That's a different rooster, another one fell on the other side of that hay bale."

"Where the hell is Amos . . . anyone seen a sprinting Lab?"

"Ya, see those roosters flying over there?"

"Ya."

"Now look at that black dot wagging its tail where the birds used to be."

"Amos, get your ass over here . . . Amos! . . . is my shock collar still in the truck?"

"Did anyone find the bird over by the hay bale?"

"Too late, Iron Jaws ate it already. . . ."

The conversation gets even better after the stalk. Sometimes I think hunters are actually fiction writers in disguise, testing their material on each other to see what passes as believable and what doesn't. For us, those post-hunt musings began at J. R.'s cozy game

J. R. Dienst flushes a pair of roosters on his Pheasant Creek Ranch near Lakin, Kansas. Kansas remains the only state in America with a four rooster limit per day—and there are enough birds to justify the generous daily bag. (Photo © by Chris Dorsey)

room. You don't play pinball in this room, you look at game mounts from around the globe. As you sit at the dining table, a greater kudu is poised within spitting distance while an African lion rests in an ideal position over your shoulder to tell if you're holding a full house or three of a kind. J. R.'s petting zoo, of sorts, is captivating and requires little in the way of feed. In their tenure on those walls, I suspect the stiff beasts have heard more lies than a Catholic priest.

J. R.'s game room seemed an odd oasis in the midst of endless farm country. It simply added to the surrealism of the entire experience. After feasting like conquering tribesmen, we returned to Lakin for the night where we slumbered at a comfortable house J. R. provides for his hunters.

We disembarked each morning for Dienst's ranch where we began the day's adventure. While I've never been one to dwell on the numbers of birds flushed, shots fired, and birds taken, I have never been in a place where those numbers—and these are wild, not planted pheasants—were nearly so dramatic. Seeing two hundred pheasants in a day isn't uncommon here and it takes three hundred flushes or more before J. R. feels as though he has something special to boast. It takes far less to impress me. Having been weaned on pheasant hunting in the Great Lakes states, to simply see two roosters on any given day was cause for celebration.

The abundance of birds in Kansas is, however, but one part of its attraction to bird hunters like me. There are mornings with a panoramic view of a valley glazed in heavy frost, the sights and sounds of dog bells and bird hunters, and the smell of burnt powder that, when brought together, become a potion creating memories to last a lifetime. I was once told that the only possessions in life worth owning are experiences. Perhaps the best experiences to own start in bird country.

North: Up Country Birds

A HUNT ON THE EDGE

My earliest recollections as a pheasant hunter start in a farmhouse in Dane County, Wisconsin. Behind that house was most of the universe as I knew it, and I knew it well. A boggy marsh comprised about half of it, while the remaining forty acres were cornfields, with hundreds of acres of additional corn connected to it in someone else's universe. Though I didn't know it at the time, it was a special place.

I awoke to the sound of cackling pheasants in the mornings beginning in spring and continuing until fall. Occasionally, a rooster or two would stray from the adjacent cornfield, wandering into our backyard. One morning, when I was thirteen, I stepped out the back door to witness my young setter halfway out of his dog house, pointing a brilliant cock bird standing ten paces from him, in the midst of our mowed lawn. It was the morning before opening day of pheasant season. In spirit, I return to the back porch at that moment in time almost every October. I find myself wishing my old setter could return with me.

We logged innumerable hours exploring the back marsh together, both of us learning the ways of pheasants. To hunt pheasants in the northern and eastern states, a hunter needs a bird dog as surely as he needs the will to hunt. There is little stumbling into pheasants here, there aren't the volumes of birds you might find in the heart of the farm belt.

A person who claims that bird dogs cannot talk is a person who simply does not know how to listen. A bird dog is, as much as anything, an accurate translator—able to interpret the difference between yesterday's pheasant scent and the aroma of bird tucked under switch only three paces upwind.

If you want to learn of pheasants, spend a day afield with an experienced bird dog. While the duck hunter relies on his retriever to recover downed mallards, and the grouse hunter wouldn't be without his pointer, both hunters would still enjoy encounters with their preferred game even in the absence of their dogs. A northern pheasant hunter without a dog, however, is no more likely to find a pheasant than is a fox without a nose.

Conventional wisdom among many pheasant hunters, though, holds that even the dogless hunter can unearth ringnecks if the hunter is accompanied by his brothers, brothers-in-law, father, uncle, father-in-law, and cousins—as is often the case on opening weekend. If no dog can be found, drive the beasts from the corn. These human combines then comb row upon row in an effort to extract the pheasants. With the brigade afield, it's only a matter of counting the steps to the next pheasant.

Ironically, it is this sort of intensive ambush in the early season that leads many of the most ardent pheasant hunters I know to

Late-season pheasant hunting in the north means snow. Dogless hunters are at little disadvantage to hunters with dogs because they have only to track a pheasant until it flushes. Fresh snow makes the job even easier, because it erases all old tracks. (Photo © by Mark Kayser, South Dakota Tourism)

simply forego the opening weekend of the season, choosing to avoid the early season shooting spree found on public hunting grounds from Minnesota to Michigan. There's a fervent anxiousness as noon whistles blow from rural firehouses across my home state of Wisconsin, proclaiming late in October of each year that it's once again time for the pheasant hunt to commence. Almost as suddenly, the whistles blow themselves out and the early hunters—many of them dogless—trade their Remington pumps for Sony remotes. The rest of us, then, are left with the cattails and fencerows to ourselves. Most hunters up north fail to realize that pheasant hunting often improves as the season enters its waning weeks.

The lack of competition in the uplands leaves a solitary feeling over the brushy draws and marshlands that typically comprise the theater of northern pheasant hunting. During pheasant season, I often used to forego Friday classes at the University of Wisconsin in Stevens Point so that I could make the two hour drive south to pheasant country on Thursday night in time to hunt on Friday morning. Later I learned not to schedule classes on Friday during the fall semester. I swung by my brother's place where my setter was kept, untethered him, and headed for a rendezvous with Keith Gilbertson, a lifelong friend who also happened to be heir apparent to the best pheasant marsh in the county.

I've lost track of many old friends, but Keith isn't one of them. He is one-third bird dog, one-third salesman, and one-third diplomat. In short, he gained access to more property than Patton. He was the product of a good Lutheran upbringing, and the fact that he was related to half the county didn't hurt our chances of getting access. With his disarming smile and an innate sense of the people, who could refuse the two of us "chasing a few birds," as Keith would tell it? Though many of the local farmers seldom saw any birds, Keith did. He spent his off hours patrolling backroads, carefully monitoring the progress of the corn harvest in order to find a marsh that might be full of birds, pushed to the cover by combines from the surrounding cornfields. I provided the dog and he secured the property—a symbiotic relationship if ever there was one.

A typical weekend was comprised of an exhaustive search for ringnecks. We often started by hiking Hansen's marsh, a pocket of cover in a sea of corn, with a railroad bed running through the midst of it. An evening hunt several years back was particularly memorable.

"The roosters will fly out of the corn just before dark," said a confident Keith, "just wait, you'll see."

But, with the sun nearly over the horizon, no birds cackled in the isolated marsh. We sat for nearly an hour waiting for the cocks to fly from the corn, crowing their arrival as they flew. It wasn't an altogether uncommon occurrence early in the year, but that was

Wisconsin hunter Phil Brodbeck and his two-year-old setter startle a rooster along the edge of a cornfield. Standing cornfields serve as reservoirs, holding birds throughout the winter. (Photo © by Chris Dorsey)

State workers release pheasants onto public hunting areas in Wisconsin. These birds provide much of the hunting here and elsewhere. (Photo courtesy Wisconsin DNR)

before hunting pressure turns the ordinarily vocal birds into mutes. It seemed like a viable tactic, however, given that there were thousands of acres of standing corn surrounding the marsh, and it would be impossible for us to cover the property before dark.

"I'll call 'em in," he said.

"You'll what?" I asked.

In that instant, Keith opened his mouth as if priming a guttural belch. The sound that came out of his mouth, however, was that of a rooster. He had refined the call after years of listening to pheasants around his house. Before I could finish chiding him for his attempt, a pair of roosters took flight from the corn and landed within two hundred yards of us.

"I told ya," he said between laughs, fully as amazed by the birds' reaction as I was.

We marched to the birds whereupon my setter quickly pointed one, then the other. I took the first bird, letting Keith flush the second bird in front of the staunch setter. Our field strategy couldn't have been better planned by Schwartzkopf and, until the point that Keith made the flush, execution was superb. After emptying three 12-gauge loads, though, Keith returned home birdless. The riches of that afternoon, though, were found not in birds in the bag, but in carefree laughter at a single moment in time—a simple time in our unfettered lives.

Some of our most important concerns revolved around our pursuit of pheasants. Mapping strategy on how we might best hunt his marsh, for instance, was serious business—picture several generals hovering over a transparent map of a battlefield. It was, however, essential that any strategy brought us back to his house by noon, where June, his mother, would have a heaping lunch awaiting us.

These weren't cold-cuts-on-white-bread lunches. A pot roast smothered in potatoes, carrots, andonions, and salad, rolls, and gravy would get us started. I could have feasted on the aromas of June's kitchen alone. She was relentless in her cooking, often shoving hot pie and ice cream in front of us. We had no recourse but to eat it. When finished—when there was no more food on the table—we rolled off our chairs and into the living room where we sprawled out like lumpy snakes in a desperate attempt to take the pressure off our stomachs. The pheasants were safe for another afternoon.

Pheasant hunting was never more fun. Come to think of it, life was never better, either.

Iowa: Down on the Farm

ARE PHEASANTS WORTH MORE THAN CORN?
Picture a big white house with a porch that stretches halfway

Iowa continually boasts one of the largest pheasant flocks in the country. The state is also home to good quail hunting in its southern two tiers of counties.

around it. Imagine an old Allis Chalmers tractor sitting under a shed made of a makeshift roof stretched between two corn cribs. Behind the shed is a small, wooden-fenced corral about the size of an Olympic swimming pool. Inside the pen stand six Herefords, eight hogs, and a scattering of chickens, each bird scratching through steaming cowpies in search of undigested grain. A 1963 Chevy, rusted to its tires, leans against a barn attached to the corral. Behind the barn is a graveyard of deceased farm equipment—antiques to the city folks, useless junk to the farmer. Around the base of the house, the farmer has piled bales of straw for added insulation against the fierce winds that blow across Iowa each winter. It could be any farm in these parts.

This is the face of Iowa farm country that Norman Rockwell never painted. Perhaps it didn't exist when he brushed his famous portraits. Maybe he, like so many Americans, however, didn't care to notice the other side of farm life. This is the reality where not even twelve-hour workdays are long enough. There are creditors who circle the land like vultures, waiting to foreclose on a mortgage the same way the devil snatches a soul.

Today, though, Iowa farmers are discovering that pheasants, which once were little more than a natural byproduct of their less-than-efficient farming, are a valuable commodity. The increased demand for pheasant hunting and shrinking crop prices led, in the mid-1980s, to the natural birth of an organization called Pheasants Galore, based in Corning, Iowa.

It is a unique guide service that pairs hunters with Iowa farm families who provide bed, breakfast, and a place to hunt for a fee. The concept is the brainchild of Darwin Linn and Bob Manke, a pair of enterprising Iowans who saw a way for farmers like themselves to earn a return on the game birds raised on their property. The idea has been well received by both farmers and nonresident hunters alike, and probably couldn't have come at a more opportune time for either.

Iowa farmers—like so many across America's breadbasket—were scrambling to save their way of life at a time when the nation's farm economy was at a record ebb. In many cases, even the relatively small amount of money provided to farmers by nonresident hunters can make life on the farm much more comfortable. It can often be the difference between full and empty stockings at Christmas.

I made the journey to Iowa with Chuck Petrie, an outdoor journalist and editor from Wisconsin. Usually, editors are good people to hunt with because they spend much of their lives looking at fine print and, therefore, cannot see very well. They are little competition for the first shot at a flushing rooster. Chuck, however, is an exception to the rule, and despite his need for bifocals, he is a fine wingshot.

Chuck and I were lured from our Wisconsin homes because our state had long since ceased being party to plentiful pheasant numbers. Our host for three days of hunting was the Leo and Betty Palmer family of rural Corydon, Iowa. They accepted us as though we were relatives dropping by for a weekend visit. Much is made of Southern hospitality, but Iowa farm people are the ambassadors of middle America. Bringing hunters into the homes of Iowa farm families creates something of a cultural exchange: It gives hunters a better understanding of the farmers' plight, and at the same time farmers are given insight into the motivations of hunters. This interchange is important in a time when too many farmers and hunters have come to see each other as enemies.

The only enemies facing hunters in Iowa, however, are some dense patches of blackberry and other nearly impenetrable thorn-bushes. But what were a few thorns to a pair of savvy grouse hunters like us?

We awakened each morning to the smell of bacon, eggs, and

Multiple flushes aren't uncommon in Iowa's best pheasant country. This Conservation Reserve field yielded two-thirds of an Iowa daily bag of pheasants. (Photo © by Chris Dorsey)

coffee permeating the Palmer homestead. Our hunt commenced in mid-December, and the winds from an Alberta clipper were howling, threatening to blow the house down with every breath, as we sat at the kitchen table.

Gary, Leo and Betty's son and our Pheasants Galore hunting guide, unfolded his county map on the table as we sipped coffee, plotting strategy in an impromptu briefing. I didn't particularly care what the map said, I was perfectly willing to let Gary lead us to the riches of birds in the vicinity. Having hunted the areas around his home farm since boyhood, he knew exactly where to take us. There would be no time lost in asking permission to hunt or finding productive cover. Finally, we wrapped ourselves in jackets and proceeded to face the wind and the day's hunt.

Within moments of arriving at our first stop, my ten-year-old setter, Thor, slowly walked the stiffness out of his legs, reminding me of an old man getting up from a soft sofa. The years haven't been kind to his joints, but his nose was as pure as ever. It was only seconds before he stiffened again. This time, though, it wasn't arthritis—it was bird scent that caused his paralysis. From beneath the canopy of an Osage tree flushed a covey of perhaps a dozen quail, thereby unlocking the old dog from his stance. A bobwhite fell to my shot, and Chuck gleaned two more from the covey with the help of his side-by-side. Petrie's bovine-sized Labrador, Baxter, rooted through the cover to pluck out the ill-fated bobs.

Much of the thrill of hunting in areas where you might find two or more species of game birds comes from reading your dog. To the casual observer, there is no difference in the way a dog follows one scent or another. To the dog's owner, however, the difference can be striking. It is the same way that a parent can distinguish between his or her child's voice and that of hundreds of other children. Thor will sprint after a running rooster in an attempt to loop in front of the bird and coax him into stopping his run to freedom. Quail seldom elicit such a response from the savvy setter.

We ended our morning hunt at a casual pace—the best way to hunt—and engulfed our lunches. I have been forever fond of mixing the flavor of cheese and crackers on my palette. I shook the thermos of hot chocolate and poured half a cup into the lid and sipped it, both hands cupped around it to extract every BTU possible. We looked like German troops standing on the Russian front in January, steam rising from our breath like smoke from a cigar.

Following the interlude, we targeted a series of brushy draws that meandered through the property until they climbed to a confluence at a large, flat field of harvested corn. The heavy cover in the draws served as a funnel, concentrating the running birds as we worked uphill to the coverless field where the birds would have to flush. The grass in the draws served as a sort of reservoir for birds, with the cover strips that led to the field effectively serving as feeder

Iowa's lengthy pheasant season provides plenty of opportunity to enjoy both early and late season hunts. Dogs are a necessity to locate pheasants in large tracts of Conservation Reserve set-aside. (Photo © by Dodd Clifton)

Weed-choked draws and ditches along the edges of crop fields provide ideal hideouts for ringnecks. These Iowa hunters are hunting on land leased by Pheasants Galore, a guide service based in Corning, Iowa, that caters to out-of-state hunters. (Photo © by Chris Dorsey)

streams. As we neared the top, a coyote, resplendent in its thick, winter pelage, dashed from the cover and raced across the open field. The pheasants followed close behind, flushing in twos, threes, and fours as Baxter worked his way to the top of the draws. As Chuck neared the edge of the upper field, he flushed a flock of ten pheasants and executed a beautiful left and right double on a pair of departing roosters.

That night, after a couple of cocktails and dinner in Corydon, Chuck and I returned to the Palmers' for a well-deserved night of sleep. We aired the dogs one last time for the night and put them up in their warm travel kennels in the back of the truck. It was time for bed. Little did we know that Leo was waiting for us to watch the University of Iowa basketball team play the Ohio State Buckeyes on TV. Iowa ball teams are revered in that state more than new tractors, and, in spite of being foot sore and wind whipped, it was difficult not to share Leo's enthusiasm as we stayed up to watch Iowa beat Ohio State 83 to 75.

The next morning, as we ate breakfast, hundreds of Canada geese alighted in small flocks in Leo's back pasture. Petrie, an inveterate waterfowl hunter, alternately eyed the birds from the patio window, and then me, contemptuously, over the tops of his bifocals, across the kitchen table. The Iowa waterfowl season closed the week prior to our arrival. I had set the date for our Iowa pheasant hunt, and the thought of waterfowl hunting hadn't crossed my mind.

"A little more planning on someone's part," Chuck muttered, "might have made this the trip of a lifetime. I'm reminded of the time grouse hunting in Wisconsin when you strolled into one last piece of cover and said you'd catch up with me at the truck. I walked three miles to get it and ended up picking you up where I left you. But," he smiled, "I'll find it in my heart to forgive you if you give me the first shot at every bird that gets up today."

Well, of course, I didn't, but over our last two days in the Corydon area, I didn't have to. We had the fields to ourselves and never saw another pheasant hunter during our three-day stay. And the hunting was splendid. Pheasants and bobwhite quail were concentrated in the wind-protected draws and swales. The dog work, by Thor, Baxter, and Gary's two German shorthairs, was exceptional in the cold weather. The company—the humor, the conversation, the Palmers' hospitality—was unsurpassed.

On the afternoon of our last day in the field, Gary, Chuck, and I were walking out of a large CRP field planted to foxtail. Our game vests were filled with legal limits of pheasants and several quail, our memories with tales to last for years. As we coursed the cover back to the truck, however, pheasants began to flush wildly ahead of us like the grand finale of a Fourth of July fireworks display. It was a send-off you could expect only in Iowa.

Recipes for Preserves

"Both he and the Prince of Wales (King Edward VIII) shot with Lord Burnham on the record day in December 1913 when nearly 4,000 pheasants were killed. In the train going home, the Prince of Wales noticed that the King was unusually silent. At last he said quietly, 'Perhaps we overdid it today.'"—Jonathan Garner Ruffer, The Big Shots—Edwardian Shooting Parties

Recipes for Preserves
The Different Faces of the Game Farm Hunt

"Not 'dummy' birds, but explosive, high-quality, genetically true ringnecks, nationally known and used to complement native hunting." This advertisement appeared in a national sporting periodical and tells much about the state of game farm hunting. The game farm in the ad was hoping to distinguish its birds and hunting conditions from those found at other clubs. By so doing, the ad, in effect, was saying that not all game farms are created equal.

Ideally, a game farm should closely approximate hunting found in the wild. You'll know you're experiencing a quality game farm hunt if, even for a moment during your hunt, you forget you're at a game farm. The difference between an enjoyable game farm hunt and a cheap imitation is often the degree to which farm managers pay attention to all the components of a quality hunt. What, then, are the different facets of a worthwhile game farm hunt?

Birds are the most important part of any game farm hunt. Without birds that look and fly like wild pheasants, there is no way to provide a quality experience. When hunters of yesteryear thought of game farm pheasants, they envisioned birds whose tails had been pecked to mere stubs, birds that even had difficulty flying. Today, however, thanks to modern poultry science, commercially raised pheasants commonly look, sound, and fly like their wild counterparts.

Almost as important as the birds to a game farm hunt is the

cover in which they are hunted. If the habitat in which you are hunting is beaten-down and empty shot-shells litter the ground, it is difficult to imagine that you are enjoying a quality hunt. Conscientious farm managers continually rotate the areas where hunters are allowed to roam, thus reducing the trampled look to the land.

Moreover, hunters should be given enough room to wander without having to compete with other hunters. Good game farms give the impression that you have the whole property to yourself, allowing you to explore cover at your own pace. Bird pens, dog kennels, and any other items that suggest a game farm should be located out of sight from areas where birds will be released for hunters. You don't truly appreciate the value of a quality game farm hunt until you have experienced a poor substitute.

For the person removed from the country, a game farm can be the next best opportunity to be afield with dogs and birds. Many successful game farms and shooting preserves rely heavily on urban clients to spend a portion of their city earnings in the hunt clubs' rural atmosphere. Such places are also good locales in which to introduce youngsters to hunting in a controlled environment. The idea isn't to mislead the new hunter into believing that game farm hunting is the same as hunting on other public or private properties. The point is to create enthusiasm for the sport. Too many kids, unfortunately, get their first taste of pheasant hunting during opening day on a crowded public hunting area. Hunters there may argue over who shot a given bird, others leave the field cursing their dogs in frustration over their unfruitful efforts—there is little reason for the newcomer, subsequently, to look forward to another such hunt.

In addition to the value of game farms as first stops for young hunters, they are increasingly being used by corporate America as meeting centers. Several shooting preserves now cater especially to

This hunter enjoys a driven pheasant shoot in the wilds of Hungary. Driven bird shooting is rife with tradition throughout Europe, but has not gained the same appeal in America. (Photo © by Stan Warren)

business executives who may wish to reduce the stress of high-level decisions by placing themselves within the comfortable environs of a hunting club. It's sort of the back-to-nature approach to business. Poets throughout the ages have extolled the virtues of being surrounded by the soothing wild. Inspiration, they lobby, comes from time in open spaces. I don't think it's stretching the idea to suggest that sound decisions are more likely to come from people who spend time thinking among trees and fields.

The lengthy seasons found on shooting preserves are yet another reason this kind of hunting has gained popularity in recent years. While seasons set by state game departments have grown shorter in many cases, and bag limits have become increasingly restrictive, game farm seasons typically last five months or longer and a daily take is commonly only limited to the number of birds you wish to purchase. A group of hunting partners who want to introduce their bird dog pups to more pheasants than can be found in the wild will also schedule post-season outings at a game farm or preserve. In an era when access to private land is increasingly difficult, game farms have become the modern alternative to driving country roads seeking a landowner's permission to hunt.

GAME FARMS AND PHEASANT INTRODUCTION PROGRAMS

In recent years, state-run game farms have been used not only to provide the masses of hunters who frequent public hunting grounds with targets, but in special breeding programs designed to produce new populations of self-sustaining, wild pheasants. In Michigan, for instance, biologists searched for a way to halt declining pheasant populations and went to China's Sichuan province for the answer. It is here where the Sichuan pheasant resides.

Michigan biologist Pete Squibb headed the international

The take from one day of driven bird shooting can number into the thousands—depending on the number of guns and availability of pen-raised pheasants. These birds are displayed in ceremonial fashion, complete with pine boughs around them. (Photo © by Stan Warren)

Driven bird shooting is just that. It's shooting—not hunting. Birds are raised and released for the sole purpose of conducting the shoot—which can offer some of the most demanding pass shooting you will ever encounter. (Photo © by Stan Warren)

Large pheasant hatcheries like this supply breeders from around the country with day-old chicks. Pen-raised pheasants still represent a major percentage of the birds hunted each fall. (Photo courtesy Don Bates, Wisconsin DNR)

project that culminated with a shipment of eggs from the Sichuan province to East Lansing, Michigan, some ten thousand miles from their home in the People's Republic of China. The eggs hatched a new era of pheasant management in the 1980s for the Wolverine State.

Squibb and others concurred that the Sichuan pheasants—proven remarkably adaptable in their native land—would be wise choices for release in Michigan. The state's game farm was the natural place to raise the birds and begin a breeding program whereby subsequent generations could be released into the wild. Initial returns on the radio-tagged birds that have been released indicate an excellent survival rate in their new environs in rural Michigan. The state has plans to continue stocking the birds, increasing the numbers released each year.

Like Michigan, Wisconsin has also begun dabbling in pheasant futures. State biologists were able to acquire pheasants from the

Modern facilities at the Wisconsin state game farm insure a high survival rate of birds raised in captivity. The state-of-the-art brood buildings provide a disease-free environment in which to raise the birds. (Photo courtesy Don Bates, Wisconsin DNR)

These young pheasants have been fitted with blinders to prevent them from pecking other birds. Pheasants are cannibalistic, and birds will often kill weak birds of the flock. (Photo courtesy Don Bates, Wisconsin DNR)

Jilin Province of China through a private game farm connection in the state. Wings Over Wisconsin, an organization comprised mostly of sportsmen, funded the project, centered over a ten-square-mile area in eastern Wisconsin.

The Chinese birds were selected from a region located in the same latitude as Wisconsin and where land use is similar to that found in the Badger State. The primary crop in the Jilin Province is corn, so the birds are expected to easily adapt to their new environs in Wisconsin. Unlike most of the pheasants released in the eastern U.S., the Sichuan and Jilin pheasants liberated in Michigan and Wisconsin will be direct descendants of wild stock and it's hoped they'll add to the genetic diversity and survivability of the states' existing pheasant flocks.

DRIVEN TO SHOOT

Game farms have been used for over a century to provide royalty—and in recent years those who simply had large disposable incomes—with the pleasure of driven pheasant shooting. Make no mistake about it, driven shooting is not hunting. The shooter remains in a small blind—called a "butt" in Europe—and practices his pass shooting prowess on birds that are flushed his direction by a band of drivers and their dogs.

The concept of the driven shoot developed in the mid-nineteenth century when wealthy landowners in England entertained guests brought to the countryside by the newly constructed railroad lines. In one historian's words ". . . you combine the opportunities of a . . . machine-gunner with an infinitely better lunch."

Enormous amounts of money were spent to see that shooters were entertained during the event. An entire British social structure developed thanks to the new influence of the people who sponsored driven shoots. Though driven shoots never made their

Michigan biologists are hopeful that the Sichuan pheasants will quickly adapt to their new environs in the Wolverine State. The birds from this province were selected because of the similarity in climate between Sichuan Province and the state of Michigan. Initial findings indicate that the birds are acclimating well to the Midwest. (Photo © by Pete Squibb, Michigan DNR)

way to America—at least not in the same sense that they were popularized in Europe—they still exist throughout the Continent. Driven red grouse and pheasants remain available in the Scottish highlands. Exquisite dinners in castles and bagpipes on the moors can be a part of the driven shooting experience there.

British driven shooting means pheasants by the truck load. Game farms provide the fodder of pheasants—sometimes thousands each day—for massive shoots. Hundreds of people may be involved in the huge undertaking. Game keepers, drivers, loaders, and shooters each follow a protocol refined from decades of practice.

In Spain, shooters have the opportunity to test their pass shooting skills on the country's population of red-legged partridge. Driven pheasant shooting can also be had in Hungary, one of the Continent's most beautiful nations.

A shooter buying a position in a driven shoot buys a package

Chinese volunteers collect eggs from the nests of Sichuan pheasants in the Sichuan Province of China. The eggs were collected for shipment to Michigan where they will provide the seed for a new stocking experiment. (Photo © by Pete Squibb, Michigan DNR)

experience that begins with unequalled shooting opportunities and ends with plush lodging and unmatched dining. Shooters purchase such hunts (available through some U.S. travel agencies) for many the same reasons people take high-dollar cruises or other vacations. Prices are commensurate with the labor-intensive nature of the driven shoot and the resources expended to sponsor such an event. But for the person who lives to shoot and whose pocket is deep, driven shooting can be a personal look at what was once a sport reserved for nobility.

A Nose Full of Desire

"THE DOG'S NOSE IS THE BIRD HUNTER'S EYE. MANY HUNTERS
WHO CARRY A SHOTGUN IN SEASON HAVE NEVER LEARNED TO
WATCH THE DOG, OR TO INTERPRET HIS REACTIONS TO SCENT."
—ALDO LEOPOLD, A SAND COUNTY ALMANAC

A Nose Full of Desire
Pheasant Dogs
from Boykins to Weimaraners

Imagine a pheasant hunt without a dog. Now think of fishing line without a rod and reel. Ostensibly, it might be possible to catch fish without them, but when the separate parts are worked in concert, the odds of success are far better. The same is true for the hunter who goes afield with a well-trained bird dog.

Perhaps no other bird is more difficult to hunt without a dog than the ringneck, for no other upland game bird can run quite like a pheasant. It wouldn't come as a surprise to me if, in about another thousand years, the pheasant would evolve into a wingless beast, with drumsticks like that of a turkey, able to withstand hours of continual sprinting. Some of these freaks may already exist in a couple of my favorite haunts, places where seemingly the same birds have run from three generations of my gun dogs.

Great pheasant dogs are judged by their ability to cope with these running birds. The pointer that sweeps promising cover until the scent wafting from a bird becomes so intense that the dog stops, signaling to the hunter the location of the bird, is the incarnation of the ideal pheasant pointer. The perfect pheasant flusher, on the other hand, traverses cover fast enough to prevent pheasants from escaping on foot, but slow enough to allow the hunter to remain within shotgun range.

The act of pheasant hunting is more than a matter of birds in hand, however. It is an aesthetic experience, a sensual smorgasbord where the sight of a pointing dog loping through cover, the sound of its rhythmic bell, the smell of goldenrod, and the feeling of exuberance are intertwined. Without one ingredient, the flavor isn't complete.

Of course there are the practical concerns and the conventional wisdom that tell us that fewer birds are lost if a hunter uses a bird dog while afield. There are the game department statistics from Kansas to Pheasantdom that document the improved success hunters with dogs enjoy over those who, with pity, have no dogs. I have never given much heed to statistics—unless, of course, they support my case—but my richest memories afield are the moments spent casting in unison with a setter that could read my mind. For me, there need be no other reason to hunt with a dog.

A DOG FOR YOU

Dog trainers are forever advising hunters to pick a pup based on the birds they intend to hunt. Standard lines go something like this:"If it's southern quail you're after, consider a pointer, and if that doesn't work, try a different pointer and, if at last you still can't find birds, hire a trainer for your pointer."

"For pheasants, look no further than a flusher—probably a spaniel," say most.

"If you can't have a setter," many grouse hunters are often told, "any of the close-working pointing varieties will do."

To my way of thinking, however, it makes far more sense to select a dog that will conform to your style of hunting. Picture an older, overweight bird hunter trying to keep pace with a whip-tailed pointer that crosses county lines in the time that it takes most dogs to cross the street. It might be that the pointer is an exceptional bird-finder, but the hunter might not be as good at finding his dog. Such a hunter would be better served and would save innumerable headaches if only he'd found a dog he could cope with, for if the

This ten-week-old English setter owned by Phil Brodbeck is pointing pigeons as part of an early introduction to birds. Though serious field training is normally preceded by weeks of yard lessons, it's helpful to develop a dog's bird sense at an early age. (Photo © by Chris Dorsey)

hunter can't control the dog, there will never be peace while afield with it.

Look carefully at yourself: Are you capable of a brisk pace through pheasant cover? Do you prefer a slow, methodical gait in which you can comb every bit of a small area? Would you rather a dog only hunt the cover that looks the most promising, quickly moving on to better looking habitat? Do you want a dog that's a full-time family pet and a part-time hunter? How do you define style in a bird dog and is it important to you? Would you rather hunt behind a flushing breed or a pointing dog? How much time do you have to spend in training your pup or will you hire a professional trainer? These are only a few of the questions you will need to answer before choosing the dog that is right for you. Here, then, is a personal account of the breeds and their general characteristics—perhaps there's a pup waiting for you.

A choice of bird dog, like the making of a friend, can bring lasting enjoyment. The author and his aging setter take a moment between covers. (Photo © by Keith Benoist)

They're all cute at this age. Selecting the dog for you, however, is a complicated task. You must first define what you need in a bird dog before you seriously consider any breed. (Photo © by Chris Dorsey)

The pointer—formerly called the English pointer—is an intense bird finder. While pointers have the potential to be truly great pheasant dogs, some may range too far to be effective for most hunters. (Photo courtesy Ralston Purina Co.)

CONTINENTAL BREEDS

These are the breeds most often referred to as "versatile" hunting dogs for their ability to point birds as well as retrieve downed game. The term "continental" is derived from the European ancestry of these breeds, which include the German shorthair, vizsla, Weimaraner, German wirehair pointer, pointing griffon, Brittany, and pudelpointer.

The German shorthair and, to a lesser extent, the German wirehair have gained much North American notoriety in this class.

Professional dog trainer Bob West steadies a young setter in a training session. When selecting your pup, look for these characteristics in the pup's parents: "nose," desire, cooperation/bidability, self-confidence, and a strong pointing and retrieving instinct. (Photo courtesy Ralston Purina Co.)

The hallmark of the continental breeds is their blue-collar, no-nonsense approach to game. There is nothing flashy about these breeds, but they tend to be close working when compared to their setter and pointer counterparts. If you prefer a slower pace in a pointing dog, one of these breeds might be your choice. They will work cover meticulously, and many I've hunted with have proven to be extremely reliable bird dogs that are easy to direct while afield.

Like the German shorthair, the Brittany has won a steadfast

Selecting the right dog food for working dogs is important if you want success. Here, Bobby McGee, a research technologist at the Purina Labs, weighs feed portions for various nutritional studies conducted at the center. (Photo courtesy Ralston Purina Co.)

following of hunters who favor close-working pointing dogs. The Brittany also sports a heavier coat than do most of the continental breeds, which makes it even more popular among northern pheasant hunters who require that a dog withstand cold temperatures while afield.

SETTERS AND POINTERS

Of the three breeds of setters—English, Irish, and Gordon—only the English setter has gained widespread appeal among hunters.

Kansas author Mike Pearce prefers golden retrievers—like his veteran Mysti, pictured—for close-in pheasant work. Goldens are as functional as they are handsome. (Photo © by Chris Dorsey)

This seven-year-old Chesapeake Bay retriever is owned by actor Jameson Parker, and is as effective in the uplands as he is in the water. Though seldom used by pheasant hunters, this breed has all the attributes needed to make a fine pheasant dog. (Photo © by Chris Dorsey)

Springer spaniels like this veteran pheasant dog owned by Wisconsinite Scott Reinert have gained an avid following among pheasant hunters because of their close-working, no-nonsense approach to game. (Photo © by Chris Dorsey)

This German shorthair has located a pheasant in a California field. Shorthairs are close-working pointing dogs that excel at both finding pheasants and retrieving them when they're downed. (Photo © by Chris Dorsey)

While the pointer has become the dominant field trial breed in North America, the English setter remains a popular breed for pheasant and grouse hunters. The long, thick coat of the setters, like that of the Brittany, often makes them a better choice for the colder climates of the northern regions. Setters typically work cover with a stylish gait, head high, searching air currents for bird scent.

Within the classification of English setter there are two distinct varieties: the bench—or show—setter and the field setter. Bench setters are typically much larger than their field counterparts, some weighing eighty pounds or more. An average weight for a field setter will normally be between forty and fifty pounds. There has also been much cross breeding between the bench and field setters with the hope being, of course, to produce a handsome setter that can also hunt. The results have been well mixed.

The Irish setter, and a hybrid version now called the red setter, follow next in order of popularity among upland bird hunters. For years, the Irish setter was bred for its sleek good looks in the show ring. In the process, however, breeders developed a narrow-headed, scatterbrained setter whose mind didn't seem to have room to log information on birds and bird hunting. The era of the hunting Irish setter was born again, though, when hunters and field trialers infused blood from English setters and pointers into Irish setter bloodlines, creating the new red setters.

A few breeders even introduced English setter and pointer blood to the black-and-tan-colored Gordon setter. However, despite a few of these experimental breedings, the Gordon bloodline has retained its genetic integrity. These beautiful dogs have a loyal constituency who want to hunt behind a stylish, close-working pointer. The breed is still relatively uncommon in the states and Canada, but if you're willing to search dog periodicals, you will undoubtedly find one.

The antithesis of the Gordon is the pointer, formerly called the

German shorthairs—along with other continental breeds such as the Brittany, German wirehair, and vizsla—are often termed "versatile" because of their ability to retrieve as well as point many different species of birds under varied conditions. (Photo © by Denver Bryan)

When hunting thick cover like this cattail slough, it's important to have a dog that can negotiate dense vegetation and water. The value of a dog that will make water retrieves isn't fully appreciated until you hunt with a dog that will not swim a ditch to fetch your bird. (Photo © by Denver Bryan)

English pointer. These dogs are half bird-finders and half speed merchants, blowing through cover like dust devils. When it comes to locating birds, no breed does it better than the pointer. Though the pointer is most popular with southern quail aficionados, there are scores of pheasant hunters who fancy them as well. While the pointer is unparalleled in its pointing ability, they aren't nearly as well known for their retrieving attributes—though I've hunted with several that performed the task admirably.

RETRIEVERS

For many the word retriever means, simply, Labrador retriever. There are, however, several fine hunters in the retriever class: golden, Chesapeake Bay, curly-coated, and flat-coated retrievers, as well as the Irish water spaniel.

The Labradors—black, yellow, and chocolate—have an enor-

Experienced pheasant dogs soon learn to grasp downed roosters by the back, avoiding the sharp spurs of a cock pheasant. This Brittany aptly demonstrates the technique. (Photo © by Denver Bryan)

The Brittany's intensity and bird-finding ability make it a superb choice for hunters who prefer close-working pointing dogs. Its orange and white coloration also makes it highly visible in the brown drab of most covers. (Photo © by Denver Bryan)

mous following and with good reason. Aside from being superb all-around retrievers, most are fine upland hunting dogs as well. Despite all this, it is the pleasant disposition of the Lab that makes it popular with hunters and nonhunters alike. Labs are tremendous family pets and are notably gentle with young children. Labs are also easily trained, which is one reason they are commonly used as seeing-eye dogs.

Not to be outdone, the golden retriever is also an exceptional bird finder and fetcher. I've hunted with two—one a Kansas whizbang by the name of Mysti and the other a veteran Montana hunter—that were as effective a pair of pheasant dogs as I've ever run across. Both were equally fine family pets and versatile water retrievers as well.

A Chessy, Max, owned by actor Jameson Parker, grabbed my attention in a Kansas pheasant field when it came to a staunch point at the end of a field of sorghum. Three of us stood only feet from

The stylish gait of the English setter and its keen nose and intelligence have made it a favorite among many pheasant hunters. Its warm coat makes it suitable for colder northern climes. (Photo © by Denver Bryan)

the pointing Chessy and wondered exactly what it was doing—obviously it didn't know that it was supposed to simply flush the birds. Jameson, equally surprised by his dog's behavior, walked in front of Max and flushed a hen from under the dog's nose. In addition to the novelty of its pointing behavior, the strong beast could work through even the thickest cover, unearthing pheasants. Chessys often have a reputation of being possessive and sometimes aggressive dogs, though you would never know it from the gentle disposition of Max.

SPANIELS

Ask most professional dog trainers to name the breed that they would most recommend hunters purchase for the purpose of pheasant hunting and they will most often answer the springer spaniel. These happy-go-lucky flushers make short, sweeping casts in front of the hunter and vacuum available bird scent. They are quick to learn and can be effective hunters during their first year afield. They don't require the consistent and persistent training often associated with the pointing breeds and, like the Labradors, make splendid pets. Beyond the springer, the other spaniels have yet to gain wide acceptance among hunters. It isn't, however, because of a lack of hunting ability. The American water spaniel, English cocker spaniel, and Boykin spaniel all exhibit strong hunting instincts, but only their lack of exposure to a wide cross section of bird hunters explains why more of them aren't used by hunters.

Flushing breeds like the golden retriever pictured above are only an asset if they locate birds within range of the shotgunner. Veteran pheasant dogs learn not to waste time on old scent, concentrating instead on birds nearby. (Photo © by Chris Dorsey)

Making the Shot

"SHOOTING THINGS OUT OF THE AIR IS A COMPLEX ACTIVITY; THE
MORE WE TALK ABOUT IT, THE MORE WE ANALYZE IT, THE MORE
COMPLEX IT BECOMES. . . . THE MORE COMPLEX IT BECOMES, THE
MORE WE FEEL WE MUST THINK ABOUT IT, THE LESS SUCCESSFUL WE
ARE AT BUSTING FEATHERS OR CLAY."
—LIONEL ATWILL, SPORTING CLAYS

Making the Shot
What Makes a User-friendly Gun?

Pheasant hunting is an athletic endeavor. Stomping through brush, hurdling bogs, and wading through cattails is the upland hunter's decathlon. The last thing a pheasant hunter (or hiker) wants to tote is a heavy gun, thus further straining already weary back muscles. The idea of the sport is to have fun, and lugging an obese shotgun is anything but fun.

There was a time, though, when a typical off-the-rack shotgun sported a thirty-inch barrel and was choked full. Those same heavyweight shotguns—some weighing nine pounds or more—have been replaced by a new generation of guns weighing under seven pounds. These new models are also shorter and more easily maneuvered.

The big guns, like oversized gas-guzzling autos, outgrew their markets and have become as antiquated as the nickel beer and the Studebaker. Although many of these guns of yesteryear still find use today, the evolution of shotguns has brought smaller, lighter armament.

Gun weight is an important attribute that hunters ought to consider when selecting a gun for the uplands. The best fit and smoothest swinging gun will mean little if your back aches and your arms are tired from the heft of your shotgun. It makes little sense, then, to carry a heavy shotgun when there are so many better options available.

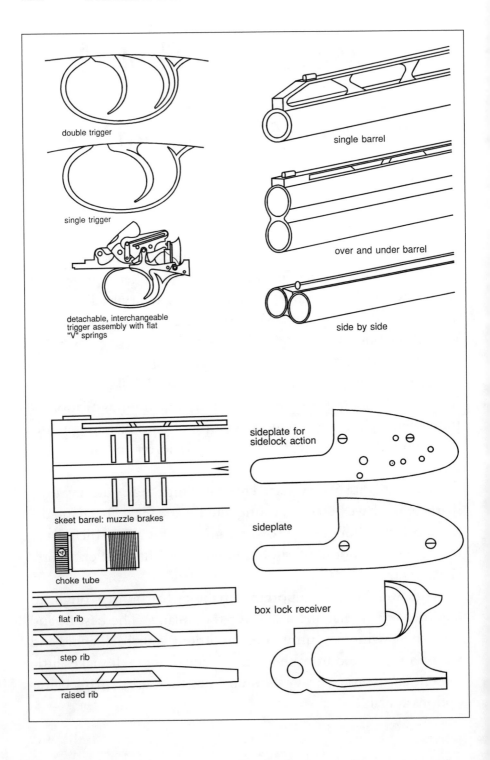

double trigger

single trigger

detachable, interchangeable
trigger assembly with flat
"V" springs

single barrel

over and under barrel

side by side

skeet barrel: muzzle brakes

choke tube

flat rib

step rib

raised rib

sideplate for
sidelock action

sideplate

box lock receiver

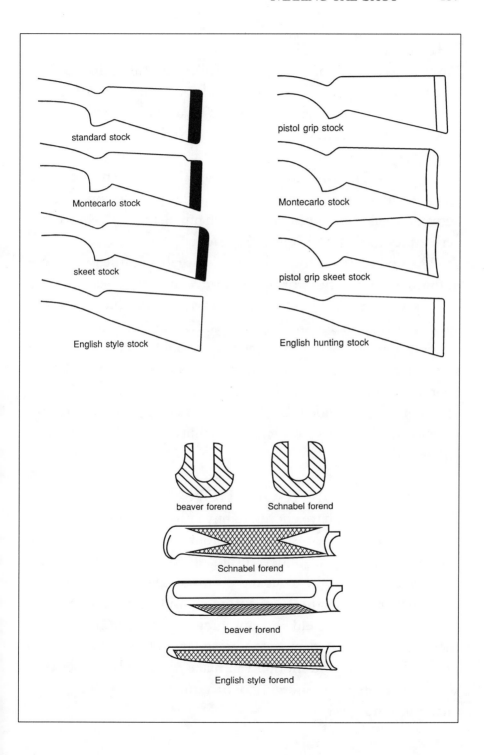

standard stock

pistol grip stock

Montecarlo stock

Montecarlo stock

skeet stock

pistol grip skeet stock

English style stock

English hunting stock

beaver forend   Schnabel forend

Schnabel forend

beaver forend

English style forend

THE RIGHT GAUGE

This brings us to choice of gauge. While everything from a .410 bore to a 10-gauge has been used to take pheasants, the 12-gauge is to pheasant hunting what the sweet 20-gauge is to quail gunning. There are those, however, who will suggest that nothing is better than a 16-gauge for pheasants, and they can make a logical case for such a choice. The 16-gauge, they argue, falls midway between the 12- and the 20-gauge, thus making it the perfect compromise between what some consider too much punch in the 12-gauge and perhaps too little power in the 20-gauge.

The popularity of the 12 and 20 is largely because of the ease of finding ammunition for them. If on a far-away pheasant foray you—gasp—happen to run out of shells, a country store is far more apt to stock 12-gauge shells than it is, say, 16-gauge or 28-gauge ammunition. Following the same logic, would you drive a vehicle that ran on gasohol unless you were sure you could find fuel? Moreover, both the 12- and 20-gauge have proven to be effective pheasant guns, provided the shooter knows how to use them, so it isn't as if a hunter is sacrificing the ability to take birds by using either gauge.

THE RIGHT CONFIGURATION

Assuming that you have chosen to buy either a 20- or a 12-gauge, you will also want to consider one of four standard configurations: side-by-side, over-and-under, autoloader, or pump. The double-barreled guns—side-by-sides and over-and-unders—typically are more expensive than their semiautomatic and pump counterparts. Purists wouldn't be afield with anything but a double gun, though their decision is based more on personal aesthetics than it is on practicality, for a good shooter can make most shotguns perform well, but even great shotguns won't turn a lousy shot into a champion shotgunner.

Within the double gun category, there are several different grades of shotguns that may cost as little as three hundred dollars or as much as a home in the suburbs. These pricey doubles—sometimes called high-grade or "best" guns—often represent the work of fine gun artisans, people who fashion their armament with the same precision with which a Steinway is built. It isn't necessary, however, to acquire a second mortgage to support your shotgun habit. There are functional shotguns to fit every budget and taste; you have only to seek to find the one for you.

THE RIGHT CHOKE

Once you've chosen one of the four configurations available, you have the task of selecting barrels with the correct chokes for the job. Until 1870, that wasn't an option as all shotguns were constructed with cylinder-bore barrels. Fred Kimble, a creative market hunter from Illinois, is credited with developing the first primitive shotgun chokes. That is, if you want to believe the American version. You see, the British claim that one of their gunsmiths, W. R. Pape, was the first to constrict shotgun barrels in 1866. While the debate is intriguing, you should know that shotgun chokes have evolved dramatically since the nineteenth century.

Hunters today have several different chokes from which to choose, though these three are the most common: improved cylinder, modified, and full choke. If you were to shoot at a paper bull's-eye forty yards away, improved cylinder would theoretically have the fewest pellets within the bull's-eye, while full choke would have the most. Modified choke, then, would fall somewhere in between. Improved cylinder, it is said, has the most "open" of the three chokes and should throw between 45 and 55 percent of a shell's pellets into a thirty-inch circle at forty yards. Modified choke will have between 55 and 65 percent of the pellets in the circle. Full choke, finally, will throw 70 to 80 percent of its pellets in the same size circle at an equivalent distance. Simply put, improved cylinder is the choice of close-range wingshooting since pellets spread to a wider pattern at a shorter range than do the same pellets fired from a full-choked shotgun. In contrast, birds flushing at long range may require a "tighter" pattern, thus a modified or full choke is then a better choice.

To test a gun's chokes, simply pace off forty yards from a large, clean sheet of white paper with a dot drawn in the middle of it. After shooting your shotgun at the dot, draw a thirty-inch circle, using the dot as the center point of the circumference. You'll then want to determine the number of pellets in the load. Keep in mind that there are roughly 135 No. 4 pellets, 170 No. 5s, 225 No. 6s, and 350 size 7½ pellets to the ounce. Simply multiply the number of pellets per ounce for the size shot you are using by the weight of the shot load in ounces. Now, divide the number of pellet holes you counted in the thirty-inch circle by the number of pellets the shot load contains. The result will give you the percentage of your pattern that is within the thirty-inch circle.

In double shotguns, most pheasant hunters favor one barrel bored improved cylinder and the other modified choke. With the advent of interchangeable choke tubes, however, hunters have the option of mixing and matching different chokes to suit the shooting conditions of the day. These interchangeable choke tubes can simply be screwed in or out of the end of a shotgun's barrel or barrels, thus eliminating the need to change guns each time you want to change your effective killing range.

THE RIGHT LOADS

Selecting a choke for your shotgun, though, is a decision that is naturally related to the kind of feed you wish to give it. While I have come to favor 1¼ ounces of No. 6 shot propelled by 3¾ drams (equivalent) of powder, there are any number of shot and powder combinations that will be effective for pheasant hunting. Shotshells of today, like present-day chokes, are enormous improvements over those of a bygone era. Old–time shot was very soft and would greatly deform while being propelled through the barrel. Shot innovator John Olin, however, discovered that by increasing the amount of antimony in the lead used for pellet production, the shot was less apt to deform in the barrel and thus provided more consistent patterns.

There is also much speculation that the nontoxic (steel) shot that waterfowlers are required to use may eventually be required for upland bird hunting. While many upland bird hunters fume at such a notion—since many believe that steel shot, if fired through some guns, will destroy their barrels—there are a few alternatives to the hard steel shot currently under development. A shot made of a tungsten alloy reached testing stages in Europe, and other types may soon follow. At present, however, there is uncertainty as to whether or not the shot will fulfill the U.S. Fish and Wildlife Service's requirements to be considered "nontoxic," and the alternative tungsten shot is expensive to produce.

For now, your choice of shotgun, choke, and shell should be made after a thorough review of your needs and wants. Here, then, is a look at some popular shotgun models from which you might choose your next upland special.

Winter cover is especially important to pheasants in the northern fringe of their range. Heavy snows typically bury seeds and spilled grain, making standing cropfields and heavy cover critical to pheasant survival. (Photo © by Ron Spomer)

Proper gun fit is achieved when the shooter's pupil aligns perfectly with the bead of the gun. Through a series of measurements, a skilled gun dealer can fit you with a gun. Here, Mike Murphy shows an over-under to a potential buyer at his store in August, Kansas. (Photo © by Chris Dorsey)

Over-under, side-by-side, pump, and auto-loader—shoot them all before choosing your next pheasant gun. (Photo © by Chris Dorsey)

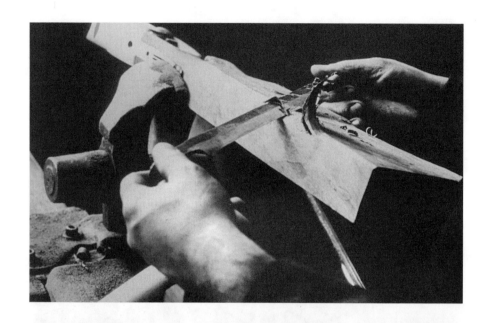

Above: Selecting the wood for a high-grade double shotgun takes both skill and experience.

Above left: Here a gunsmith begins roughing what will be the stock for yet another fine Beretta shotgun. The company still employs Old World craftsmanship in the making of its guns.

Below left: Engineers employ sophisticated computer-assisted design and manufacturing programs to continually improve gun design at Beretta.

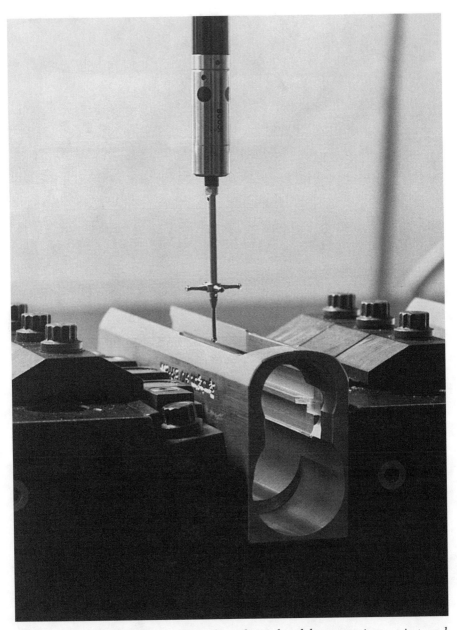

At Remington's coordinate measuring machine, the machined shotgun receivers are inspected by an electronic sensor that also records and stores a receiver's serial number.

The "Pheasant Tower" is a great station in which to test your skills at simulated driven pheasants. This station is part of a rapidly growing sport called sporting clays. This British game has gained many followers in the states because it approximates wingshooting better than any other clay game. (Photo © by Chris Dorsey)

Above: *Specialized clay target throwers and clay birds have been developed especially for sporting clays. Here, the author loads the "Fur and Feather" station in which one target is bounced along the ground to simulate a bolting rabbit, while the other target is flung in the air in a simulated crossing shot. (Photo © by Dave Hetzler)*

Left: *In sporting clays, the shooter must remain in the station while shooting, and the thrower may delay the release of the clay birds up to three seconds after the shooter calls for them. (Photo © by Chris Dorsey)*

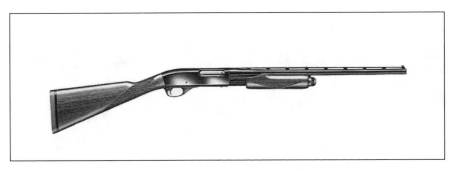

Remington's popular Model 870 Special Field features a twenty-one-inch vent-rib barrel and English-style straight-grip.

Remington 870 Special Field: Though Winchester's Model 12 was the pump shotgun of yesteryear, today's best known pump is Remington's Model 870. This venerable shotgun is offered in several variations, but the straight English style hunting stock of the Special Field has made it a favorite among ardent upland hunters. Its smooth function, coupled with an affordable price tag, also accounts for this pump's popularity.

The 1984 release of this sleek, light-weight pump is the latest in a long line of guns from America's oldest gunmaker. The company's roots can be traced to 1816 when Eliphalet Remington crafted a handmade flintlock at his forge in Ilion, New York, beginning over 175 years of gunmaking tradition. Though the early guns were heavy and cumbersome, the Special Field is compact, featuring a twenty-one-inch barrel, a slimmed and shortened forearm, and Rem-Choke tubes. The gun weighs only 6¾ pounds in 12-gauge and a mere 5¾ pounds in 20-gauge. Both 12- and 20-gauges are offered with three-inch chambers.

Beretta Onyx Series: These field grade boxlocks come in both 12 and 20 gauge and combine traditional Beretta over-and-under and side-by-side designs with some special features made to appeal

Beretta's Onyx Series of double shotguns features American walnut stocks, Mobilchoke screw-in choke system, and automatic ejectors. Barrels are offered in either twenty-six- or twenty-eight-inch vent rib.

to American shooters, such as American walnut stock and forearm, recoil pad, screw-in chokes, and automatic ejectors. All Onyx shotguns feature Beretta's black weather-resistant semi-matte finish to reduce glare and improve heat dispersion and anti-corrosion qualities. Both the over-and-under and side-by-side models are available with twenty-six- or twenty-eight-inch ventilated rib barrels.

While American gun manufacturers have long been recognized as the makers of the finest rifles in the world, European double shotguns hold the same status in the world of shotguns. This Italian company was created about 1500 by Bartolomeo Beretta, making it the world's oldest industrial enterprise. The plant is located in Brescia, Italy's gunmaking capital. The Val Trompia mountains north of Brescia are home to many venerable gun makers: Franchi, Gamba, Zoli, and Bernardelli. Although Beretta operates a plant in Accokeek, Maryland, most of the company's shotguns are still crafted in the Old World.

Browning BPS Pump: The BPS offers bottom loading, bottom ejection, and a top tang safety. This may truly be the only "ambidextrous" pump on the market. While lefties such as myself

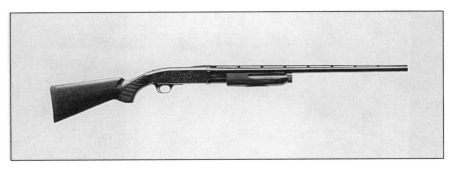

Though Browning offers a variety of pumps and doubles, this engraved version of the BPS is popular. The gun's unique feature is its bottom loading and ejecting design.

have forever endured right-handed pumps as a fact of life, the BPS is equally functional for either the left- or right-handed shooter. A side-ejecting pump will fling shells across a left-handed shooter's line of sight, but the bottom ejecting BPS does not.

The BPS is offered in several configurations, from those that are engraved to the functional Upland Special. Like Remington's Special Field 870, the Upland Special comes with a twenty-two-inch barrel and is lightweight for fast swinging. The 12-gauge version of the Upland Special weighs 7½ pounds while the 20-gauge is only 6¾ pounds. Some shooters find these guns too light and have difficulty swinging them smoothly on a flying target. The virtue of such lightweight armament, however, is found at the end of a day of long-distance hiking when a bulky gun will seem as though it's made of lead.

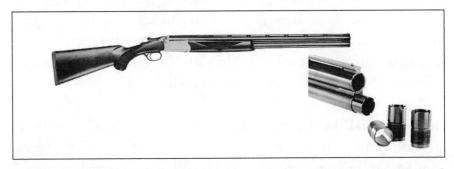

The Ruger Red Label remains the only American made over-under shotgun. Its functional design and affordability have made it a frequent choice of pheasant hunters.

Ruger Red Label: The Red Label is currently the only American made over-and-under shotgun on the market. The functional design (which includes heat-treated and blued chrome-molybdenum steel on the trigger guard, top lever, safety thumbpiece, and on the barrels of the gun) coupled with its affordability, has made this gun popular among American pheasant hunters. This boxlock is chambered for three-inch shells, comes with either twenty-six- or twenty-eight-inch barrels, and weighs about 7½ pounds. Screw-in chokes are also available for all 12-gauge models.

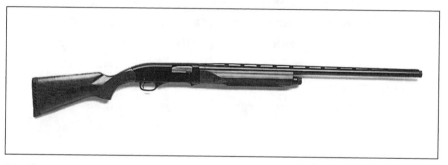

Winchester's fine auto-loader, the 1400, sports a twenty-eight-inch barrel with Winchoke. Auto-loaders have an avid following among many pheasant hunters.

Winchester Model 1400 Semi-Auto: Winchester semiautomatic shotguns come in several configurations, and the Model 1400 is a superb choice for pheasant hunting. The self-compensating gas-operated action is fast, smooth, and reliable—rare traits in many auto-loading shotguns. The gas activated piston absorbs shock and reduces felt recoil, allowing the shooter to stay on target for accurate follow-up shots. The shock-absorbing piston is largely the reason the Model 1400 has gained its reputation for smooth shooting. The front-locking rotary bolt is machined from solid chrome molybdenum steel and locks directly into a chrome molybdenum steel barrel extension by means of four big locking lugs. The 1400 is chambered for 2¾-inch shells and has a convenient bolt-closing release.

The Perazzi Sporting Classic is another of a long line of famous Italian double guns.

Perazzi Sporting Classic: Though most Perazzi shotguns are made for competitive shooting, their Sporting Classic model is a handsome over-and-under made specifically for hunters. The gun sports 28⅜-inch barrels, a nonadjustable selective trigger, and weighs 7¾ pounds. The gun comes standard with screw-in chokes and can be used for clay target games or carried on your next pheasant hunt. This boxlock continues the long tradition of fine Italian doubles, and would be a functional addition to your upland arsenal.

The side-by-side Gentry is a Spanish-made double that is imported by American Arms.

American Arms Gentry: This side-by-side boxlock features an engraved frame, double triggers, and extractors. It is a European double made to American Arm's specifications and comes standard with a walnut stock, pistol grip, cut checkering, vented black rubber recoil pad, and a semi-gloss finish. The barrels are blued steel with monoblock construction and are made with hard chrome-lined bores that are suitable for steel shot. It's offered in 12-, 20-, 28-gauge, and .410 bore with fixed chokes. The 12-gauge version weights six pounds, fifteen ounces and has twenty-six-inch barrels.

Dressing for Success

"SHOULD PHEASANT RISE, BE MOST PARTICULAR—HE RISES NEARLY PERPENDICULAR."—OLD PHEASANT HUNTER'S VERSE, AUTHOR UNKNOWN

Dressing for Success
Selections from the
Pheasant Hunter's Closet

My hunting uniform used to consist of blue jeans, leather work boots, a tattered flannel shirt, and a baseball cap. During the early years of my pheasant hunting career, I hardly noticed the wet feet I always seemed to have after a day of marsh hopping. Inconveniences like cold hands and feet, it seemed to me, were simply a part of being a hunter—as integral to the experience as toting a shotgun or crossing a fence.

About the time I grew tired of having soggy toes and blackberry-bitten thighs, however, I discovered an L. L. Bean catalog. The days of dew-soaked pants and leaky boots have made me appreciate quality gear the same way it's more fun to drive a Mercedes after having driven a Yugo.

What follows is an outline of items that have made my forays into pheasant country infinitely more comfortable. Before you venture afield again, consider what you might be missing.

BRUSH PANTS AND CHAPS
Replacing my faded blue jeans are brush pants. I've owned scores of pants advertised as brush busters—guaranteed to be thornproof, waterproof, and "goof-proof." Some performed as promised, others couldn't survive the constant serration of blackberry patches, each thorn set like hungry sharks' teeth waiting to rip through any fabric entering the herbaceous jaws.

Because prime pheasant cover is inherently dense from a

There is a wide assortment of special clothing and gear available to today's upland bird hunters. While most gun shops—like that of Michael Murphy & Son's pictured here—offer a selection of bird hunting apparel, many hunters choose to buy by mail order instead. (Photo © by Chris Dorsey)

hunter's waist downward, quality brush pants must have certain virtues. A heavy, thorn-resistent fabric like nylon should cover the front of the pants. Without the protection of tight-weave fabrics, thorns will poke their way to your knees and thighs. Today there are a seemingly endless variety of brush pants from which to choose.

Perusing a Cabela's, L. L. Bean, Dunn's, or Gander Mountain catalog illustrates the many styles on the market today. When purchasing the garments, however, carefully inspect the stitching of the pants. Any loose threads will unravel when tested in heavy brush, thus weakening the seams. A waterproof lining, such as one made of Gore-Tex™, OmniTech™, or a similar fabric, is essential if you plan to stay dry.

Another option in legwear for upland hunters is a pair of chaps. These are particularly handy because they can be slipped off as soon as you're done hunting. I use heavy leather chaps if I'm treading through thorn country and opt for the lighter nylon variety if traipsing grassy cover.

JACKETS AND VESTS

The revolution in hunting clothes hasn't stopped with the advent of better brush pants and chaps. Well-designed vests and upland shooting jackets have also made the pheasant hunter's life more comfortable. Because of specialized tailoring and increased attention to ergonomics, shooting clothes have evolved from what were often sleeved gunny sacks to form-fitting apparel.

There are several different styles of vests for early season hunting. They range from light mesh to heavy cotton and, like similar jackets, typically have shell loops sewn onto them. Although most jackets and vests are made with elastic loops that are meant to carry shells, these loops tend to stretch and wear out within a couple of seasons of heavy use. Leather shell loops, however, are far more durable and will normally last the life of the jacket.

A generous game pouch that is lined with a stain resistant fabric is a must for both vests and jackets. Grass and twigs are forever accumulating in the bottom of game pouches, so the best pouches are designed to zip open for easy cleaning. I've also found that large front pockets are essential to carry an assortment of small items ranging from dog bells to shooting gloves to extra shells. Front-loading game pouches are also a handy design, allowing the hunter to store a pheasant without first having to remove the jacket to access the pouch.

FOOTWEAR

Pheasants seem to have a fondness for water. I have shot as many pheasants in what looked like good duck habitat as I have in what is often referred to as the "uplands." GoreTex™-lined leather

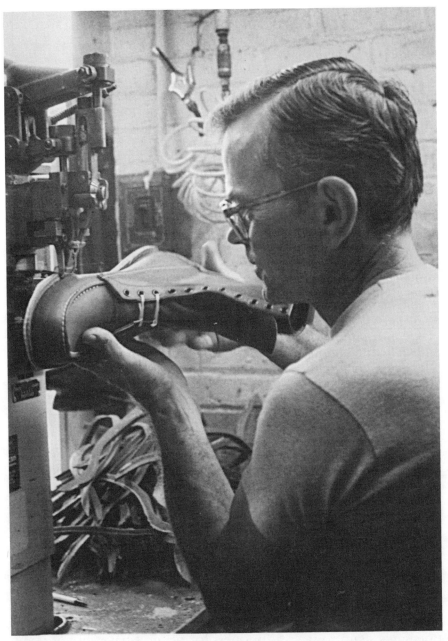

The production line at the Red Wing Shoe Company turns out several models of fine upland hunting boots. Boots for pheasant hunting must be as comfortable on dry land as they are waterproof in the wetlands. (Photo courtesy Red Wing Shoe Company.)

Brush pants made of durable fabric covered with a facing of nylon make superb pants for even the toughest pheasant cover. Many hunters, however, prefer to wear nylon or leather chaps afield. (Photo © by Denver Bryan)

boots will likely keep water out, but they probably won't do it as well as rubber boots, nor are they likely to last as long. It wasn't long ago that it was impossible to find rubber boots that fit comfortably. Most offered little ankle support and poor traction. Today, though, a number of manufacturers offer calf-high, flexible rubber boots that are ideal when hiking cattail marshes in search of ringnecks.

For those who must have leather, however, be certain to select a boot that is lined with GoreTex™ or another water-repellant fabric. Hidden creeks and bogs often stand between you and your pheasants. Any leather boots should be treated regularly with silicone, mink oil, or another waterproofing agent to protect them. Water will eventually destroy the leather, but you can slow the process by continually maintaining it.

Vibram™ soles, on the other hand, will help protect the arches of your feet. Pounding frozen dirt clods or rocky ditchlines is hard on both your feet and back, and good soles prevent excessive shock to your frame.

HATS AND SHOOTING GLASSES

Since only cock pheasants are legal game in most instances, you must distinguish between hens and roosters in order to identify your target. To that end, shooting glasses that block the sun's glare are an important aid when a pheasant flushes sunward. Such glasses also protect your eyes from snapping twigs and branches, as well as from flying debris that might come from a shotshell when it's ejected from your gun.

Hats and caps will further shield glare from the sun and will also help protect you from tree thorns and sharp sticks. As with all upland clothing, blaze orange should be the color of choice. It is impossible to be too visible while afield, and there is mounting evidence that wearing orange does indeed reduce your chance of being accidentally shot.

Vests with easy-access shell loops are ideal for early season hunts. Most shell loops that are made of elastic tend to weaken and lose effectiveness before similar loops made of leather do. (Photo © by Denver Bryan)

Detachable game bags allow hunters to carry several birds at a time and can be removed for easy cleaning. Vests and jackets made of blaze-orange fabrics have gained popularity in recent years because they have proven to reduce the number of accidental shootings among hunters. (Photo © by Denver Bryan)

Waxed cotton clothes, like these pants, vest, and hat sold by Lewis Creek, have gained a foothold in the American market because of their waterproof nature and all-around durability. Waxed cotton sporting wear has long been popular in England, but has only recently found its way to the U.S. market. (Photo © by Dave Hetzler)

GLOVES

Tight-fitting leather gloves have become a mainstay with me throughout the bird season. Specialized shooting gloves allow you to maintain your sense of touch; thus, you can operate the safety and trigger without delay. They will also protect you from barbwire and even the needle-sharp spurs of a pheasant. I once dropped a wounded pheasant that I was clutching in one hand when it suddenly came to life and spurred me. The bird scampered into a cornfield, never to be seen again. Perhaps only a *dead* bird in hand is worth two in the bush.

LANYARD AND COMPASS

Though it is rare to get lost in open pheasant country, a thick fog can make your navigation, well, more interesting. I have been, let's just say, turned-around for awhile even on my own back forty when a milky fog shrouded the land. It is an altogether disheartening feeling to be disorientated on land with which you thought you were intimately familiar. Most hunters like to admit that they have been lost while afield about as much as they like to confess to forgetting to load their shotgun as a pheasant sails unscathed out of sight. Yet the hunter who has never been at least temporarily lost is probably the hunter who has never ventured far from his car.

Evidently the problem is more common than most hunters are willing to admit since there are several companies that sell lanyards complete with dog whistle and built-in compass. These are helpful devices that can be purchased inexpensively. Small pin-on compasses are also available and can be attached to your vest or jacket.

A Pheasant in Every Pot

"WE'D NEVER KNOW THE JOY OF . . . PHEASANT WITH SAUERKRAUT
AND SAUSAGE IF IT WEREN'T FOR THE SHOTGUN." —GENE HILL,
"OUR WORLD WITHOUT SHOTGUNS"

A Pheasant in Every Pot
From Under Grass to Under Glass

"It tastes like chicken." That's how people who taste pheasant for the first time often describe their experience. Of course, that comment is often used to describe the flavor of everything from rattlesnake to rabbits. To a skilled pheasant cook, no words are more horrifying.

"Chicken!" the cook cries. "I suppose you would think lobster tastes like crayfish . . . baked Alaskan like baked potatoes, and you probably wouldn't know the difference between Ruffles and truffles?" Indeed, beware of the "C" word in the presence of a pheasant cook.

In the final analysis, pheasant is, however, faintly similar in taste to the chicken. Ringnecks have long, deeply muscled breasts of white meat. Their legs, like that of the chicken, are dark meat, though often much leaner than their domesticated brethren. The strings of a pheasant's muscle fibers are thin and fine textured, which allows the meat to remain moist while cooking despite a very low fat content.

Unlike many other upland game birds—such as quail, woodcock, snipe, and the like—a pheasant provides enough meat to make a meal for two. When dressed and ready for the oven, a typical rooster weighs an average of about 2 pounds. The natural flavor of the pheasant is exquisite, and the meat can be used in a wide variety of recipes.

FIELD CARE

Old bird-hunting doctrine says that you should pause the moment you shoot a pheasant and eviscerate the bird to allow the meat to cool quickly. The faster the meat cools, conventional wisdom argues, the better the flavor of the meat. In my experience, there is no such thing as bad pheasant. I almost never eviscerate the bird immediately in the field unless outside temperatures are particularly warm and I plan to be afield for several hours.

Upon returning home, I finish skinning the birds and remove the entrails before soaking them overnight in a cold bowl of refrigerated saltwater. The brining solution draws the remaining blood from the meat, thus preparing it for cooking or the freezer. If you decide to freeze your birds, you may choose to filet the breast meat off the bone to reduce the amount of space occupied in your freezer. Heavy, sealable freezer bags are all the necessary protection the meat needs while in the freezer, though you may want to add a wrapping of freezer paper around the plastic bags as additional insurance against freezer burn. Add water to the bags so that there isn't any air space surrounding the meat, which is the primary cause of freezer burn.

Before you cook or freeze your birds, remove as many remaining BBs as possible. Simply take the sharp point of a filet knife and poke it into the opening of a BB trail into the meat. You'll eventually cut to the BB, removing a comet of feathers that followed it into the meat. While you'll never find all of them, the fewer the BBs, the more enjoyable the dining—it's like eating fish fillets without bones.

Favorite Recipes

Ringnecks are as handsome over toast as they are pretty in the wild. The succulent white meat of the breast and the dark meat of the legs make this game bird a treasure on the table. (Photo © by Mark Kayser, South Dakota Tourism)

PHEASANT DEVON

2½ cups cubed, cooked pheasant, pressure-cooked or boiled until well-done
2 10-ounce packages frozen broccoli spears, steamed until tender
½ cup real mayonnaise
2 cans cream of chicken soup
1 can cream of mushroom soup
1 teaspoon lemon juice
½ cup grated cheddar cheese
½ cup crushed corn flakes

Place steamed broccoli in shallow casserole dish. Arrange cubed pheasant over broccoli. Combine mayonnaise, soups, and lemon juice, and heat until mixture is liquid. Pour over pheasant and broccoli; sprinkle with cheese. Bake for 20 minutes at 350 degrees. Uncover, add crushed corn flakes, and bake for an additional 10 minutes. Serves 4.

PHEASANTS IN CREAM SAUCE

2 pheasants, chunked
1½ cups flour
salt and pepper to taste
3 tablespoons butter or margarine
3 tablespoons cooking oil
1 cup sour cream
2½ cups water
2 teaspoons celery salt
1 teaspoon garlic salt

Cover pheasant chunks in flour seasoned with salt and pepper. Brown pheasant in butter and oil. Drain excess oil. Arrange pieces in baking dish.

In separate pan, mix sour cream, water, celery salt, and garlic salt. Pour over pheasant chunks, and bake at 350 degrees for 2 hours or until tender. Baste occasionally with cream to keep meat moist. Serves 5.

QUICK CAMP HONEY PHEASANT

2 pheasant breasts, skinned
1 teaspoon salt
4 tablespoons butter or margarine
1 cup clover honey

Rub salt over pheasant breasts. Place breasts on a grill over hot coals. Brush on mixture of melted butter and honey. Cover, repeating process until honey forms golden glaze over meat. Cook until well done—usually between 10 and 20 minutes. Quick Camp Honey Pheasant is great when served with potatoes and onions fried in a skillet over the campfire. Serves 2.

MUSHROOMED PHEASANT

2 pheasants, disjointed
2 eggs, beaten
½ cup flour
½ cup butter or margarine
2 cups mushrooms, sliced
1 small onion, chopped
½ cup of additional butter or margarine (to sauté mushrooms)
2 chicken bouillon cubes
½ cup lemon juice
salt and pepper to taste

Dry pheasant pieces with paper towels and dredge them first in beaten eggs, then in flour; sauté the pheasant in butter until golden on all sides. Remove meat from skillet and sauté mushrooms and onions in butter until brown, being careful not to burn them. Replace pheasant and add bouillon, lemon juice, and seasoning. Cover and cook over low heat approximately 1 hour or until tender. Serve with wild rice and steamed asparagus. Serves 3–4.

EUROPEAN PHEASANT

4 pheasants, disjointed
½ stick of butter or margarine
4 pounds sauerkraut
3 teaspoons pepper
2 teaspoons celery seeds
½ pound salt pork
1 liter dry white wine
1 pound pre-cooked Italian sausage (keep whole)
3 teaspoons additional pepper

Brown pheasant pieces in butter or margarine. Drain kraut, and put it in a large saucepan. Add the 3 teaspoons of pepper, celery seeds, and salt pork. Pour in wine, and simmer for 50 minutes. Add pheasant pieces, and smother them in the mixture, and simmer for 1 more hour.

In a large, separate pan, place the Italian sausage; pour the seasoned kraut and pheasant over top. Simmer until pheasant is tender, about 30 minutes longer. Serves 4–6.

CHINESE PHEASANT

1 pheasant, disjointed
1 tablespoon salt
½ cup flour
1 stick butter or margarine
¼ cup soy sauce
¼ cup catsup
¼ cup honey
1 tablespoon garlic powder

Season pheasant pieces with salt, and dredge them in flour. Melt butter in skillet, and sauté pheasant pieces until golden brown. Mix soy sauce, catsup, honey, and garlic powder in a small bowl. Pour mixture over pheasant; cover and cook in preheated 350 degree oven for 1 hour. Serves 2.

ITALIAN PHEASANT

1 pheasant, disjointed
1¼ cup Italian dressing

Place pheasant in baking dish with Italian dressing. Cover and bake at 350 degrees for about 1 hour. Turn the pheasant and baste with dressing during baking to coat the bird. Serve with green salad and fresh vegetables. Serves 2.

CREAMY WILD RICE AND PHEASANT SOUP

1 pheasant
1 large onion, chopped
1 cup celery, chopped
1 pound fresh mushrooms, sliced
margarine or butter to taste
1 cup flour
2 cups cooked wild rice
12 chicken bouillon cubes
4 cups half and half

Pressure cook or boil the pheasant until it is well done; chunk meat into small pieces. In separate pan, sauté onions, celery, and mushrooms in margarine or butter until tender. Sprinkle flour over vegetables until well coated (mixture will be pasty). To the freshly cooked wild rice, add bouillon cubes. Add coated vegetables, pheasant bits, and half and half. Heat and stir to make sure the vegetables blend into the soup. DO NOT BOIL. Serves 6.

CALIFORNIA PHEASANT

2 pheasants
4 bacon slices
½ cup butter or margarine
1 cup vinaigrette (your favorite kind)
3 eggs, hard-boiled
1 green onion, finely chopped
2 bunches watercress
1 ripe avocado

Roast each pheasant with two bacon slices over breasts, and use butter for basting. Thicken vinaigrette by adding 3 yolks of the hard-boiled eggs and the finely chopped green onion. Arrange watercress on large platter. Slice avocado into thin, lengthwise pieces, and arrange the pieces over the watercress. Carve the roasted pheasant in thin slices and place on top of avocado and watercress. Pour the vinaigrette over the pheasant, and serve immediately. Serves 3–5.

Pheasants Forever

"THERE ARE PLACES I REMEMBER. . . . IN MY LIFE, THOUGH SOME
HAVE CHANGED. . . . SOME FOREVER, NOT FOR BETTER . . ."
—PAUL MCCARTNEY & JOHN LENNON,
"IN MY LIFE," MCA RECORDS

Pheasants Forever
From Fledgling to Success

The 1970s and early 1980s were the dark ages of pheasant hunting in North America. Critical pheasant habitat across the continent was being dug up, plowed under, and covered with houses and shopping malls. It was a particularly frustrating period for pheasant hunters, because as they saw their favorite coverts disappearing, there was seemingly little they could do to alter the decline.

In Minnesota, however, a pair of renaissance men, of sorts, decided they could do something about dwindling pheasant populations. *St. Paul Pioneer Press* outdoor editor Dennis Anderson and the newspaper's national advertising manager Jeff Finden attacked the problem by forming an organization called Pheasants Forever.

The decline of pheasant numbers was dramatic in Minnesota. In the 1950s, for instance, hunters there were harvesting a million pheasants each year. By the late 1970s, that figure had fallen to less than 250,000 birds annually. Other states had also seen their pheasant flocks plummet.

The catalyst that brought the idea of Pheasants Forever to public attention was Anderson's 1982 article that called for the formation of an organization dedicated to helping pheasants, pheasant habitat, and pheasant hunting. Anderson's appeal generated more mail than any other story in the newspaper's history.

On August 5, 1982, the organization went from idea to

Proceeds from banquets such as this provide Pheasants Forever with much of its annual operating budget. (Photo © by Jay Johnson)

fruition, beginning a new era in pheasant conservation. In 1983, Pheasants Forever spearheaded a Minnesota bill that called for a $5 state pheasant stamp. Today, over a half million dollars a year are generated from the stamp and the money is used by the state's Department of Natural Resources for pheasant habitat improvement projects such as planting food and cover plots critical to allowing pheasants to complete their life cycle.

Also in 1983, Pheasants Forever launched a newsletter called *Rooster Tales* to inform members about the organization's projects and purpose. In April of that year, the first ever Pheasants Forever banquet drew eight hundred people. Membership swelled to one thousand members in two chapters in Minnesota by the end of 1983.

By 1984, more chapters began in Minnesota and Iowa, bringing the total membership in sixteen chapters to three thousand people. In June of the same year, the organization initiated a billboard campaign designed to convince farmers that they could "Double our pheasant population," if they were to "delay roadside mowing until Aug. 1st."

In January, 1985, Pheasants Forever worked closely with other conservation organizations to help pass the Food Security Act of 1985, otherwise known as the 1985 Farm Bill. Far reaching conservation measures—including farmland retirement programs such as the CRP—were included in this bill, considered one of the best pieces of legislation to ever impact farmland wildlife.

By the end of 1985, chapters had begun in Michigan, Colorado, New York, North and South Dakota, Illinois, and Nebraska. Jim Wooley, an upland game biologist from Iowa, became the organization's first field representative in the same year. *Pheasants Forever* magazine was also printed for the first time in this watershed year. The organization encouraged local input from hunters whose money was spent on projects in their locales.

Six more states—Wisconsin, Wyoming, Pennsylvania, Idaho, Utah, and Kansas—formed Pheasants Forever chapters by 1986. The organization also made its first land acquisition on which to create pheasant habitat in Clay County, Iowa. In a program designed to improve habitat across the pheasant's North American range, the organization shipped over two million pounds of seed in 1986. Over $250,000 were spent in 1986 for educational programs and habitat projects for pheasants. Habitat restoration projects consisted of planting woody cover for windbreaks and shelterbelts, creating food plots in areas near important wintering areas, and planting nesting and winter cover, thus providing life-sustaining habitat for the birds.

Membership in the organization grew to 25,000 among 150 chapters by 1987. New chapters formed in Montana, Indiana, and Ohio. By 1989, chapters were added in Oregon, Washington, California, Maryland, and Nova Scotia, Canada. More than $1 million were spent on habitat projects in 1989, with an additional $250,000 spent on public education programs. The organization also helped other states such as Oregon establish an Upland Game Bird Stamp. Pheasants Forever also assisted Iowa in implementing the Resources Enhancement and Protection Program, legislation that earmarked $250 million to be spent on conservation projects from 1989 to 1999.

Today, the organization boasts over fifty thousand members and is one of the fastest growing conservation organizations in North America. Their timing couldn't be more critical. In a report requested by the U.S. Congress and published by the Fish and Wildlife Service, titled "Wetland Losses in the United States," the rapid loss of wetlands throughout the continent is graphically illustrated.

Nearly 117 million acres of wetlands or 53 percent of America's original wetland acreage has been lost. Roughly sixty acres of wetlands are lost every hour, 1,440 acres each day, and over a half million acres are lost every year.

The results have been worse for some states, ten of which have lost over 70 percent of their wetlands. It's a trend that cannot continue if pheasants and other wildlife species dependent upon these habitats are to survive. As one biologist wrote, "Sportsmen's actions, or lack of them, will determine the fate of the pheasant."

For more information on Pheasants Forever, write the organization at P.O. Box 75473, St. Paul, MN 55175.

Maybe Tomorrow

"A MAN OR A WOMAN WHO APOLOGIZES FOR HUNTING IS A FOOL. IT'S A MAN'S OR A WOMAN'S CHOICE, AND HE OR SHE MUST LIVE WITH IT."—RICK BASS, "WHY I HUNT"

Maybe Tomorrow
Dissecting the
Future of Our Sport

"... sport hunters are not leaders in conservation," asserts *Animals' Voice* magazine in a 1991 cover story, "they are impediments to it." *U.S. News & World Report* sums up the American hunting dilemma in the subtitle of its February 5, 1990 cover story: "Some 200 million birds and animals are killed annually by hunters. A bitter debate now rages: Is this legitimate harvest or a wanton slaughter?" Are hunters really "... bloodthirsty, piggish, and grossly incompetent" as *Esquire* suggested in its 1990 exposé on hunting?

Of course not. But Americans who do not hunt wouldn't know it if they read scores of popular periodicals or viewed evening newscasts that have been seduced to the editorial garden only to choose the wrong fruit—picking sides with antihunters whose argument is tempting on the surface, but rotting at the core.

The surge of animal rightists, however, is but one problem on the horizon of hunting. Human overpopulation and the resulting habitat destruction that inevitably goes with it threatens to make the debate between hunters and antihunters inconsequential. The American population has doubled since World War II. The number of people in many Third World nations has grown at two and three times that rate. Landsat satellite images beamed to us from space document the strides we have taken to swallow the earth in development. For the hunter, it has brought shrinking opportunities.

I used to return to my childhood hunting haunts, driving past cattail marshes and fields of goldenrod on my way back in time. I ended my pilgrimage a few years ago when the last of my favorite pheasant covers became just another face on a real estate brochure. Each parcel on what once was country was marked by a sale sign, swaying in the winds of change like epitaphs to the ecosystem of which I was once a part.

These losses go unnoticed by most editors and broadcasters who seek only to fuel the debate between hunters and antihunters. To that end, they focus on such dramatic images as that of a fallen bison, bloodied outside of Yellowstone, or a red fox caught in a leghold trap. They see but one chapter in what is a lengthy dissertation about humans and their relationship to the land and its wildlife.

Never mind the billions of dollars spent by hunters to secure habitat for a multitude of wildlife species. Forget the research money generated from the Pittman-Robertson tax—a tax on sporting equipment such as shotguns and other hunting gear that hunters imposed on themselves to create money for game and nongame wildlife management. Such facts make boring reading and viewing to editors and television producers who struggle to shock readers and viewers out of apathy in a game where corporate survival is determined by newsstand sales and television ratings.

Hunters, then, find themselves caught between two attacking forces: On one side there are the antihunters and the media who view hunting as a vulnerable target to exploit. On the other side, there is an increasingly consumptive public whose appetite threatens to consume the planet. To hunters, it seems a bitter irony that a generation of funding conservation projects is not enough, that they must now divert money from conservation to combat animal rightists claiming to lobby on behalf of wildlife. In a 1991 report, it was estimated that over the previous five years $15 million was

Harper's, Newsweek, U.S. News & World Report, Esquire, Reader's Digest, *and other popular periodicals have covered the struggle over the notion of animal rights in recent years. Much of the coverage has painted a dismal portrait of hunters and hunting.*

These pheasant chicks are hatching a new era in which the future of sport hunting is in question. Hunter's actions, or lack of them, will help determine hunting opportunities in the next decade and beyond. (Photo courtesy Wisconsin DNR)

spent to cope with animal rightists. Sadly, that is money that could have been spent to benefit wildlife.

At the heart of the question of who will prevail lies the future of hunting and wildlife management. It is certain that there will be no cameras rolling when the next wetland is drained, and editors will find nothing dramatic about the loss of one more species: the American hunter.

ENDLESS TOMORROWS?
Three Experts Envision the State of American Pheasant Hunting

Author's Note: I have posed this question to three authorities on the ringneck: What will pheasant hunting in America resemble in the year 2030? Noted pheasant researcher Dr. Richard E. Warner, Pheasants Forever executive director Jeff Finden, and author Steve Grooms share their views in a futuristic look at American pheasant hunting.

Dr. Richard Warner

DR. RICHARD WARNER
Dr. Richard E. Warner is the Director of the Center For Wildlife Ecology at the Illinois Natural History Survey. Since 1970, Warner has been involved with a variety of pheasant research projects, including involvement in what is the longest continuous pheasant study in the United States. He is the author of numerous scientific articles describing the ecology and management of pheasants in North America.

REACHING THE LIMIT

By recognizing current trends, the hunting of wild pheasants in the year 2030 can be described in terms of Who will hunt? Where will hunting occur? And what will these hunts be like?

Who Will Hunt Pheasants?
Pheasant hunting in America has largely occurred on privately owned farmland. Traditionally, most pheasant hunters were members of farm families or their circle of friends and relatives. The hunting population was a melting pot of society—cutting across ethnic groups, locations, and socioeconomic situations. Like the pursuit of other small game, pheasant hunting was often termed a "poor man's sport" because it was accessible to all. Hunters typically remunerated farmers for access to their land only in token ways.

However, hunting opportunities have plummeted in recent decades because the farm population has undergone considerable down-sizing, reducing the potential contacts between farmers and hunters. In addition, pheasants have disappeared in some areas, and access to land has become an issue because of heightened concerns regarding liability. These factors will still influence hunting in 2030. A large percentage of hunters will have a client relationship with landholders; hunting agreements will often be in writing, and financial remuneration will be far more than token payment. After figuring the cost of land leases for hunting, time and money spent for travel, lodging, and equipment, it will be common for hunters to spend hundreds of dollars per pheasant bagged! Only a few percent of the human population in most regions will hunt wild pheasants—a trend that is already apparent over much of the eastern and midwestern states. In fact, pheasant hunting will be more closely linked to higher income segments of the population.

Where Will Hunting Occur?
The North American pheasant range in 2030 will resemble that of the 1980s. Wild pheasants will exist in numbers sufficiently attractive to sparse numbers of hunters in portions of states in mid-to-northern latitudes, as well as in pockets of range in western and

Game farms may provide an increasing amount of hunting opportunities in the future. As human populations continue to expand, access to land will likely become more difficult, making the simplicity of a preserve hunt even more appealing. (Photo courtesy Don Bates, Wisconsin DNR)

southwestern states. Pheasants will occur in highest numbers on regions of farmland where soils tend to be highly productive for agriculture, but where there are also tracts only marginally suitable and profitable for cropping. The combination of farm programs diverting marginal land from production, and assistance from natural resource agencies and private groups (such as Pheasants Forever), will provide sufficient incentives for farmers to establish prime pheasant habitat on such tracts.

What Will the Hunt Be Like?

As discussed above, in the year 2030 most hunters will be clients, and pheasant hunts will be expensive. These hunts will also tend to be highly successful by recent standards, because in the better hunting regions landholders will have monetary incentives to produce an abundance of roosters for the bag, and because leases and informal agreements will strictly limit hunting pressure so that birds remain accessible. The high success rate of pheasant hunting, however, will bring other changes to the nature of the hunt. Future pheasant hunts will often provide opportunities to hunt other game as well, because many hunters will have traveled far and spent relatively large amounts of money, only to bag their limit of roosters quickly. In attempting to provide a satisfactory hunting enterprise, landholders will be increasingly prone to adopt put-and-take hunting, either to supplement the bag of wild pheasants, or to provide hunting of game species normally unsuited to a given region.

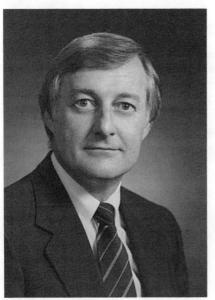

JEFFREY FINDEN
Jeff Finden served as the St. Paul Pioneer Press and Dispatch's *national advertising manager when he and outdoor writer Dennis Anderson collaborated to form Pheasants Forever, a national nonprofit organization dedicated to upland game conservation. Finden currently serves as executive director for the 50,000-member organization.*

Jeffrey S. Finden, Executive Director,
Pheasants Forever

STABILITY FOR THE FUTURE
(Dateline: Des Moines, Iowa—October 26, 2030)
Pheasant season opens this Saturday and it is anticipated that a record number of hunters will converge on Iowa's farm fields and

Young pheasants await shipment to game breeders across North America. Many private clubs raise the birds for release onto public hunting lands prior to hunting season. Such programs help state agencies defer some of the cost of raising pheasants for put-and-take public hunting. (Photo courtesy Don Bates, Wisconsin DNR)

marshes in search of one of America's most challenging game birds, the ringnecked pheasant. The Iowa Department of Natural Resources estimates the fall population of pheasants to be six million birds this season.

After its introduction into the United States in the late 1800s, pheasants flourished through the nation's agriculturally prosperous states. Their numbers peaked in the 1950s, reaching almost unbelievable populations in states such as South Dakota, which then boasted a population of sixteen million pheasants. During the next twenty-five years, pheasants experienced a dramatic decline due to changing farming techniques, urban sprawl, and intensification of agriculture that would destroy what the pheasant needed most—habitat.

Wetlands were being drained at an alarming rate and fencerows, pasture, shelterbelts and abandoned farmsteads were converted to the production of row crops. Widespread use of agricultural chemicals was accepted as the best means to enhance production. All this spelled disaster for the pheasant, and by the early 1980s population levels were dangerously low. But it wasn't only the pheasant that suffered. The intensified farming had also caused our soil to erode at alarming rates, our groundwater was being contaminated by pesticides and herbicides, and the American public was demanding Congress enact sweeping measures to deal with these and other serious environmental problems. The environment had become the most important issue in America.

Congress responded with measures to protect, enhance, and restore wetlands. Marginal farmland was idled through a program called the Conservation Reserve. Clean air and clean water bills were passed, conservation plans were in place on every farm, shelterbelts and windbreaks were being replanted, wetlands and prairies were being restored. Environmental education was mandated in school curricula. The pheasants also responded and, by the year 2000, population levels in the nation's heartland were similar to densities of the early 1960s. A balance with nature was beginning to be achieved that would allow a healthy human population to coexist with a healthy wildlife population.

In the past thirty years, pheasant populations have remained fairly stable even though the geographic range of the pheasant has diminished due largely to urbanization. This, coupled with the consolidation of family farms into large corporate units, has made hunter access on private land a great problem. Fortunately, during the late 1990s, many states in the nation's pheasant range embarked on land acquisition programs to acquire critical wildlife habitat. Those efforts, spearheaded by private conservation organizations, helped provide the numerous public areas, large and small, that we have today for hunting and other outdoor recreation. All this, thanks to the farsighted thinking of our ancestors.

Steve Grooms

STEVE GROOMS

Steve Grooms is a freelance writer living in St. Paul, Minnesota, with his wife, daughter, and two hunting dogs. He is the author of several books, including Modern Pheasant Hunting *(a "how-to" book) and* Pheasant Hunter's Harvest *(a "why-to" book). He is a field editor for* Pheasants Forever *and has published a book on the eastern bluebird. He is also currently at work on a book about sandhill cranes.*

WILL THERE BE ROOM FOR PHEASANTS?
Plotting the Course of Future Pheasant Hunts

I took my first pheasant hunt when I was three. My father loaded me and his pump in the 1940 Oldsmobile coupe and drove to the outskirts of town. Pheasants were thick enough to be a hazard to driving. Farmers, weary of crop depredation by pheasants, greeted hunters with unrestrained joy.

When I was thirteen, I was allowed to carry a shotgun. My father and I mostly hunted weedy cornfields forty miles north of town. Great flocks of pheasants clattered into the sky at the ends of our drives.

Pheasants were not so abundant when I was twenty-three. Even so, I kept a shotgun in my college dormitory and was able to walk out along some railway tracks and shoot a few roosters after my afternoon classes.

By the time I was thirty-three, our party generally drove two hundred miles to find birds. Hunting was pretty good on farms still in the Soil Bank program, though the game was tougher and we needed dogs to get birds up.

Pheasant hunting was poor when I was forty-three, even though that was the year we drove nine hours to a place reputedly rich in birds.

If one could convert those experiences to numbers and plot them on a graph, the trend would be evident. With each passing decade, I find it necessary to travel farther, pay more money, and hunt harder to find fewer birds.

One might also plot another graph. It would depict the hours I spend driving between places where I can hunt, how often other hunters screw up my hunts, how frequently requests to hunt private land are rudely rejected, and how many times I discover that a fondly remembered farm has had its cover ripped out.

At some point, the line plotting pheasant hunting opportunity

Some pheasant experts predict that hunters will be willing to pay an increasing amount of money to preserve owners for the opportunity to hunt pheasants. Here, hunters relax after a day of pheasant hunting at the Lakin, Kansas, based Pheasant Creek Lodge. (Photo © by Chris Dorsey)

With the increase in pheasant populations across much of middle America in recent years, pheasant hunting contests like this one in Wisconsin have become more common. The federal Conservation Reserve Program has created millions of acres of new habitat for farmland wildlife like the ringneck. (Photo © by Chris Dorsey)

will droop low enough to intersect the ascending line of psychic aggravation. And then I will no longer be a hunter of pheasants except in my dreams.

Will there be pheasant hunting in 2030? Very little, I think, if any. Of course, pheasants will be hunted on preserves. But that's not pheasant hunting—the birds are confused waifs trying to find their way back to the pen, and you can't "hunt" something when you already know it is there.

It goes against the grain of our culture to be pessimistic, but my life's experience does not allow me to foresee a bright future for pheasant hunting. By my reckoning, nine of ten of the places I once chased roosters are now developed or simply not worth hunting. The farmland landscape is changing in chilling ways. Every year agriculture takes on more of the character of the factory—artificial, neat, and stultifyingly uniform.

Not all trends are bad. Some states persist in investing in programs to improve bird numbers. Some farmers are managing for pheasants in order to charge money from hunters. Good hunting might be available in the future to the hunter able to pay enough for it (though I have yet to see *wild* pheasants perform well as a cash crop).

Moreover, I'm encouraged by how rapidly today's chemically dependent farming style is falling into disrepute. All evidence suggests this style of farming, so ruinous to wildlife and the land, is as unsustainable and uneconomical as it is invidious to the welfare of the planet.

But I view current human population trends with dismay. There are more people alive now than the planet can afford, with staggering increases coming. We seem compelled to wring every possible bit of food out of our tortured soil. I cannot imagine any farming technology based on maximum productivity that would have living room for pheasants.

If we are to have pheasants in 2030, there must be room in the world for a certain amount of inefficiency, for weeds and funky low places, for a bit of chaos. When every square inch of land must justify itself to bankers in pinstripe suits, what value will they place on the wild rooster who greets the rising sun with a strident yawp of defiance?

References

Allen, Durward. *Our Wildlife Legacy*. Funk & Wagnalls Company, New York, 1954.

Atwill, Lionel. *Sporting Clays*. Atlantic Monthly Press, New York, 1990.

Bateman, Robert. "The Best Things in Life are Not Free Anymore." *Pheasants Forever,* Fall 1990, 14–23.

Bowlen, Bruce. *The Orvis Wingshooting Handbook*. Nick Lyons Books, New York, 1985.

Carson, Rachel. *Silent Spring*. Houghton Mifflin, New York, 1962.

Davis, Henry P. *Training Your Own Bird Dog*. G. P. Putnam's Sons, New York, 1969.

Duffey, David M. *Bird Hunting Tactics*. Willow Creek Press, Wautoma, WI, 1978.

Etter, S., J. E. Warnock, and G.B. Joselyn. 1970. "Modified Wing Molt Criteria For Estimating The Ages of Wild Juvenile Pheasants." *J. Wildl. Manage.* 34(3):620–626.

Gates, J., J. B. Hale. *Seasonal Movement, Winter Habitat Use, and Population Distrubution of an East Central Wisconsin Pheasant Population*. Technical Bulletin No. 76. Wisconsin Department of Natural Resources, 1974.

Gates, J., J. B. Hale. *Reproduction of an East Central Wisconsin Pheasant Population*. Technical Bulletin No. 85. Wisconsin Department of Natural Resources, 1975.

Grenfell, W., B. M. Browning, and W. E. Stienecker. *Food Habits of California Upland Game Birds*. Report No. 80–1. California Department of Fish and Game, 1980.

Grooms, Steve. *Pheasant Hunter's Harvest*. Lyons & Burford Publishers, New York, NY 1990.

Hallet, D., W. R. Edwards, and G. V. Burger. *Pheasants: Symptoms of Wildlife Problems on Agricultural Lands*. North Central Section of The Wildlife Society, Bloomington, IN, 1988.

Hemker, T., J. Bryant. *Idaho Pheasant Workshop*. Idaho Department of Fish and Game. 1990.

Hill, Gene. *Shotgunner's Notebook*. Countrysport Press, Traverse City, MI, 1989.

Larson, David. "Pesticides And Pheasants in Utah." *Current Utah Pheasant Issues*. Utah Division of Wildlife Resources, 1991.

Leopold, Aldo. *A Sand County Almanac*. Ballantine Books, New York, 1966.

Norris, Charles. *Eastern Upland Shooting*. Countrysport Press, Traverse City, MI, 1989.

Proper, Datus. *Pheasants of the Mind*. Prentice Hall, New York, 1990.

Rude, Kathleen. "A Graphic Loss." *Ducks Unlimited,* March/April 1991, 20–22.

Ruffer, Jonathon Garnier. *The Big Shots*. Tideline Books, N. Wales, 1987.

Smith, Steve. *Hunting Upland Game Birds*. Stackpole Books, Harrisburg, PA, 1987.

Squibb, Pete. "New Bird From The East." *Michigan Natural Resources,* September/October 1985, 4–11.

Trautman, Carl G. *History, Ecology, and Management of the Ring-necked Pheasant in South Dakota*. Bulletin No. 7. South Dakota Department of Game, Fish and Parks, 1982.

Vander Zouwen, W. J. 1990. "State and Provincial Programs For Habitat Enchancement On Private Agricultural Lands." Pages 64–83 in K. E. Church, R. E. Warner, and S. J. Brady, eds. *Perdix V:* gray partridge and ring-necked pheasant workshop. Kansas Department of Wildlife and Parks, Emporia.

Warner, Richard. *Illinois Pheasants: Population, Ecology, Distribution, and Abundance,* 1900–1978. Biological Notes 115. Illinois Natural History Survey, 1981.

Index

About the Author

After serving as senior editor for Los Angeles–based Petersen's *Hunting*, Chris Dorsey joined the staff of *Ducks Unlimited* magazine, where he is executive editor. He is also the author of *The Grouse Hunter's Almanac* and *Hunt Wisconsin*. His freelance work has appeared in *Writer's Digest, Sports Afield, Field & Stream, Outdoor Life, Sporting Classics,* and a host of other regional and national publications. His writing has taken him to hunts in North and South America, Africa, and Europe. He began training his first bird dog pup—a Brittany—at the age of six and has raised and trained bird dogs ever since. Dorsey is a graduate of the University of Wisconsin–Stevens Point with degrees in English and Natural Resource Management. He's a Wisconsin native who now resides in Memphis, Tennessee.